The Trouble with Maths

D1330566

Now in a second edition, the award-winning *The Trouble with Maths* offers important insights into the often confusing world of numeracy. By looking at learning difficulties in maths from several perspectives, including the language of mathematics, thinking styles and the demands of individual topics, this book offers a complete overview of the most common problems associated with mathematics teaching and learning. It draws on tried-and-tested methods based on research and the author's many years of classroom experience to provide an authoritative yet highly accessible one-stop classroom resource.

Combining advice, guidance and practical activities, this user-friendly guide will enable you to:

- develop flexible thinking skills
- use alternative strategies for pupils to access basic facts
- understand the implications of prerequisite skills, such as working memory, on learning
- implement effective preventative measures before disaffection sets in
- recognise maths anxiety and tackle self-esteem problems
- tackle the difficulties with word problems that many pupils may have
- select appropriate materials to enhance understanding.

With useful features such as checklists for the evaluation of books, an outline for setting up an inclusive maths department policy and a brand new chapter on materials, manipulatives and communication, this book will equip you with the essential skills to tackle your pupils' maths difficulties and improve standards. This book will be useful for all teachers, classroom assistants, learning support assistants and parents who have pupils who underachieve with maths.

Steve Chinn is an independent international lecturer, writer and researcher. He spent twenty-four years as head teacher of three specialist schools and was a mainstream teacher for fourteen years. www.stevechinn.co.uk

The Trouble with Maths

A practical guide to helping learners with numeracy difficulties

Second edition

Steve Chinn

Routledge
Taylor & Francis Group

LONDON AND NEW YORK

First published 2004
by Routledge

This second edition published 2012
by Routledge
2 Park Square, Milton Park, Abingdon, Oxon OX14 4RN

Simultaneously published in the USA and Canada
by Routledge
711 Third Avenue, New York, NY 10017

Routledge is an imprint of the Taylor & Francis Group, an informa business

© 2004, 2012 Steve Chinn

The right of Steve Chinn to be identified as author of this work has been
asserted by him in accordance with sections 77 and 78 of the
Copyright, Designs and Patents Act 1988.

All rights reserved. The purchase of this copyright material confers the
right on the purchasing institution to photocopy pages that bear the
photocopy icon and copyright line at the bottom of the page. No other
part of this book may be reprinted or reproduced or utilised in any
form or by any electronic, mechanical, or other means, now known or
hereafter invented, including photocopying and recording, or in any
information storage or retrieval system, without permission in writing
from the publishers.

Trademark notice: Product or corporate names may be trademarks
or registered trademarks, and are used only for identification and
explanation without intent to infringe.

British Library Cataloguing in Publication Data
A catalogue record for this book is available from the British Library

Library of Congress Cataloging in Publication Data
Chinn, Stephen J.
The trouble with maths : a practical guide to helping learners with
   numeracy difficulties / Steve Chinn. – 2nd ed.
   p. cm.
   Includes index.
   1. Mathematics – Study and teaching. 2. Special education.
   3. Underachievers – Education. I. Title.
   QA11.2.C48 2011
   510.71 – dc22   2011007003

ISBN: 978–0–415–67010–4 (pbk)
ISBN: 978–0–203–80593–0 (ebk)

Typeset in Helvetica
by Florence Production Ltd, Stoodleigh, Devon

Printed and bound in Great Britain by the MPG Books Group

To Sarah

Contents

Illustrations

Figures

Tables

Preface to the second edition

It has been eight years since I started writing the first edition, which seems quite a long time in education. However, this book is about maths education and here the changes tend to be in pedagogy and philosophy rather than in the content of the curriculum. Sadly there is an underlying and resilient tendency for the changes to be regressive. The foundation for change is often, 'Don't change', because, 'What worked for me when I was at school will work for everyone'.

There is an increasing body of evidence, from many sources and many countries about what works in maths education. It was the Cockcroft report from the 1980s that inspired Singapore to create a maths curriculum that has made them world leaders. Sadly, it did not inspire the UK as effectively. The recent Sheffield report noted that we have had a tail of underachievement in maths that has been unaddressed for decades. California embarked on a traditional approach to maths that took them to the bottom of the achievement tables in the US. Telling is not teaching.

Fortunately there are two persuasive sources of objective information that can guide us towards making maths education more effective, Hattie's (2009) major review of research into education, *Visible Learning*, and the US National Research Council's (2004) book *How Students Learn*.

The first edition of *The Trouble with Maths*, written before these books were published, was structured around ideas that were very close to those in these two books. The second edition has done this consciously. Working for twenty-five years with students who found learning a challenge teaches one a lot about teaching and learning.

In the second edition I have taken out the chapter on assessment and diagnosis and replaced it with a chapter on materials and manipulatives. There will be a companion book, *More Trouble with Maths: A teacher's complete guide to identifying and diagnosing mathematical difficulties*. One of the key factors for me is that teaching has to be diagnostic and that diagnosis should guide teaching.

In this edition I have taken out all references to the UK's National Numeracy Strategy (NNS). Most maths curricula are generic and I wanted to focus on maths topics and the learning problems they may generate rather than a specific curriculum.

In each chapter I have reviewed the content and updated it in the light of recent research. For example, in the chapter on anxiety I have included my own research, both formal and informal. The informal research is perhaps the more disturbing and a key reason for writing this book. I have been asking teachers who attend my lectures, at what age are enough children giving up on maths for the teacher to notice and the modal answer is seven years old. This is across the UK and is also an international issue.

Finally, I am not trying to provide all the answers. That would be an impossible task. I am trying to highlight issues and give strategies that are flexible, adaptable and extendable.

Steve Chinn
TwMaths Ltd (www.stevechinn.co.uk)

1 Introduction: learning difficulties in mathematics and dyscalculia

This book was written to help teachers, classroom assistants and learning support assistants who deal with pupils who are underachieving in mathematics. It provides several perspectives on the situation, from preventive measures to thinking styles, to ideas for intervention. It works like a repair manual in some respects and like a care awareness manual (looking after your students) in other respects.

It is a book that can be accessed in different ways. It can provide an overview of where and how problems may arise. It offers insights into areas of potential difficulty. It can focus on a particular problem and suggest approaches that can help the pupil to learn, but it would be an impossible task to attempt to provide an answer for every problem for every child. It's a book that is more about prevention than cure. However these two facets do interlink.

It can be used to:

- understand some of the possible reasons for problems in learning maths;
- pre-empt problems;
- develop flexible thinking skills;
- circumvent problems in basic numeracy;
- address the difficulties pupils have with word problems;
- teach alternative strategies for accessing basic facts;
- recognise maths anxiety, attributional style and self-esteem problems;
- stimulate ideas for teaching maths to pupils who are facing difficulties with the subject;
- select appropriate materials and manipulatives for teaching maths topics.

Sometimes you may find information repeated in different chapters of the book. This is deliberate as some observations fit into more than one area. The new area should give a different perspective to that information.

A few golden rules

- Don't create anxiety.
- Experiencing success reduces anxiety.
- Experiencing failure increases anxiety.
- Understand your pupils as individuals.
- Be as consistent as possible; address inconsistencies.
- Teach to the individual in the group . . . also known as the 'Teach more than one way to do things' rule.
- Remember where each topic leads mathematically.
- Understanding is a more robust outcome than just recall.
- Try to understand errors . . . don't just settle for 'wrong'.

● Prevention is better than cure.
● All the above rules have exceptions.

A front page article in *The Times* of 30 December 2002, headed 'Exam stress strikes seven year olds', claimed that the Key Stage One tests caused symptoms of excessive anxiety including loss of appetite, insomnia, bed-wetting, forgetfulness and depression. These are our children!

What do learners need to be good at mathematics?

Although this book is about what to do when learners are underachieving in maths, it should be valuable to consider what learners need to be good at maths. I have two sources for this information. One is from the USSR and the other from the USA.

Krutetskii[1] presented a broad outline of the structure of mathematical abilities during school age. He specifies:

● The ability for logical thought in the sphere of quantitative and spatial relationships, number and letter symbols; the ability to think in mathematical symbols.
● The ability for rapid and broad generalisation of mathematical objects, relations and operations.
● Flexibility of mental processes in mathematical activity.
● Striving for clarity, simplicity, economy and rationality of solutions.
● The ability for rapid and free reconstruction of the direction of a mental process, switching from a direct to a reverse train of thought.
● Mathematical memory (generalised memory for mathematical relationships), and for methods of problem solving and principles of approach.
● These components are closely interrelated, influencing one another and forming in their aggregate a single integral syndrome of mathematical giftedness.

Although Krutetskii makes these observations concerning giftedness in mathematics, they are equally appropriate for competence. The reader can see where learning difficulties may create problems.

The other source is the National Council of Teachers of Mathematics in the USA, who list and explain twelve essential components of essential maths:

1 *Problem solving* The process of applying previously acquired knowledge to new and unfamiliar situations. Students should see alternative solutions to problems: they should experience problems with more than a single solution.
2 *Communicating mathematical ideas (receiving and presenting)* Students should learn the language and notation of maths.
3 *Mathematical reasoning* Students should learn to make independent investigations of mathematical ideas. They should be able to identify and extend patterns and use experiences and observations to make conjectures.
4 *Applying maths to everyday situations* Students should be encouraged to take everyday situations, translate them into mathematical representations (graphs, tables, diagrams or mathematical expressions), process the maths and interpret the results in light of the initial situation.

5 *Alertness to the reasonableness of results* In solving problems, students should question the reasonableness of a solution or conjecture in relation to the original problem. They must develop number sense.

6 *Estimation* Students should be able to carry out rapid approximate calculations through the use of mental arithmetic and a variety of computational estimation techniques and decide when a particular result is precise enough for the purpose in hand.

7 *Appropriate computational skills* Students should gain facility in using addition, subtraction, multiplication and division with whole numbers and decimals. Today, long complicated computations should be done with calculator or computer. Knowledge of single-digit number facts is essential.

8 *Algebraic thinking* Students should learn to use variables (letters) to represent mathematical quantities and expressions. They should understand and use correctly positive and negative numbers, order of operations, formulas, equations and inequalities.

9 *Measurement* Students should learn the fundamental concepts of measurement through concrete experiences.

10 *Geometry* Students should understand the geometric concepts necessary to function effectively in the three dimensional world.

11 *Statistics* Students should plan and carry out the collection and organisation of data to answer questions in their everyday lives. Students should recognise the basic uses and misuses of statistical representation and inference.

12 *Probability* Students should understand the elementary notions of probability to determine the likelihood of future events. They should learn how probability applies to the decision making process.

Picking up on Krutetskii's first point concerning the use of symbols in maths, the British psychologist, Skemp[2] wrote:

> Among the functions of symbols, we can distinguish:
>
> 1 Communication.
> 2 Recording knowledge.
> 3 The communication of new concepts.
> 4 Making multiple classification straightforward.
> 5 Explanations.
> 6 Making possible reflective activity.
> 7 Helping to show structure.
> 8 Making routine manipulations automatic.
> 9 Recovering information and understanding.
> 10 Creative mental activity.

He concludes that: 'The use of signs appears to be indispensable to the use of reason'.

So, we have some characteristics for being good at mathematics. Could one assume that deficits in all or some of these skills can create difficulties in mathematics? I know from experience that there are many reasons why someone may underachieve in mathematics and that the picture is a complex one with no single root cause. Recently the term 'dyscalculia', a specific learning difficulty in maths, has become more prominent and so a look at what dyscalculia might be may help our understanding of other reasons for difficulties with mathematics.

Dyscalculia, definitions and descriptions

Dyscalculia, a problem with learning mathematics, is attracting attention in official circles. The DfES (the UK Department for Education) has published a booklet on guidance for supporting pupils with dyscalculia (and dyslexia) in the National Numeracy Strategy (NNS). There is now a screening test for dyscalculia[3] published by GL Assessment, a book entitled *The Dyscalculia Assessment*, which is aimed at younger children, from Jane Emerson and Patricia Babtie, and an online screener 'DysCalculiUM' from the University of Loughborough. Despite this recent increase in attention, the literature on dyscalculia is sparse and the definitions are a little bland at present. I have extracted a few from various sources.

Developmental dyscalculia is defined by Bakwin (1960) as a 'difficulty with counting' and by Cohn (1968) as a 'failure to recognise numbers or manipulate them in an advanced culture'. Gerstmann (1957) describes dyscalculia (Gerstmann's syndrome) as 'an isolated disability to perform simple or complex arithmetical operations and an impairment of orientation in the sequence of numbers and their fractions'.

Kosc (1970) describes developmental dyscalculia as a structural disorder of mathematical abilities that has its origin in a genetic or congenital disorder of those parts of the brain that are the direct anatomico-physiological substrate of the maturation of the mathematical abilities adequate to age, without a simultaneous disorder of general mental functions. This definition clearly puts dyscalculia in the inherited and specific learning difficulties category.

In 1978 Magne gave a slightly more cautious explanation of a difficulty in mathematics as the low achievement of a person on a certain occasion that manifests itself as performance below the standard of the age-group of this person or below his own abilities as a consequence of inadequate cognitive, affective, volitional, motor or sensory, etc., development. The cause for inadequate development may be of various kinds. This description acknowledges that there will be more than one cause for difficulties in mathematics.

Mahesh Sharma (1980) lists the many words that have been suggested for maths difficulties, explaining terms such as acalculia, dyscalculia, anarithmetica and noting that there is no definite agreement on their use universally in the literature, that they have not been used consistently, and although there are significant differences between dyscalculia and acalculia (a complete inability to do any maths), some authors have used the terms interchangeably. He concludes that the descriptions of these terms are quite diverse to say the least.

Sharma suggests that dyscalculia refers to a disorder in the ability to do or to learn mathematics – that is, difficulty in number conceptualisation, understanding number relationships and difficulty in learning algorithms and applying them. It is an irregular impairment of ability. Thus Sharma suggests that dyscalculia is a specific learning difficulty.

Acalculia is used to label a more serious condition, the loss of the fundamental processes of quantity and magnitude estimation and a complete loss of the ability to count. This is an acquired condition.

And, finally, there is something that sounds like a missing member of the Russian royal family, arithmastenia, which is defined as a uniform deficiency in the level of mathematical abilities.

It seems that the term dyscalculia is used to refer to problems at the number level of mathematics rather than later challenges such as algebra and trigonometry.

I wrote the following for the Dyslexia Institute's journal, *Dyslexia Review*, in 2003. It is reprinted with their permission. It remains apposite for the second edition of this book.

Does dyscalculia add up?[4]

Initial ramblings

Is dyscalculia 'dyslexia with maths'?

With the publication of Brian Butterworth's *The Dyscalculia Screener* and the inclusion of dyscalculia as a specific learning difficulty in the DfES (the UK's Department for Education) consultation document for the 2004 SEN census, dyscalculia is a hot topic. This article sums (!) up my current thinking about dyscalculia. Unfortunately my current thinking is fluid. I am trying to make sense of all those factors which influence the maths learning outcomes of children and adults. So, I hope this paper may attract some responses and stimulate more research.

Since absolute knowledge on dyscalculia is in short supply I am going to construct this paper around the questions that I consider we have to investigate to reach an understanding of dyscalculia. In doing this there seem to be some very interesting comparisons between dyscalculia and dyslexia.

There are some things I know as a start. I know that dyscalculia will not be a simple construct (I think that means a psychological concept). I know that there will be many reasons why a person may be bad at maths. I know there will not be any instant or simple 'cures' because I know that there is unlikely to be a single reason behind the problem of the many, many people who fail to master maths and I know that not all of these will be dyscalculic.

I heard David Geary speak at the last IDA conference. This American guru compared our knowledge of dyslexia to being close to adulthood and our knowledge of maths/dyscalculia to being in its early infancy. This is reflected in the number of research studies done on language difficulties compared to those done on maths difficulties. As for studies on dyscalculia, they are few indeed. I think there are so many parallels at so many levels between dyslexia and dyscalculia and all that surrounds these specific learning difficulties, for example prevalence, definition, teaching methods, etiology and so forth.

We are some twenty years behind language/dyslexia studies in our knowledge and understanding of dyscalculia. This is not to say that I think it will take us twenty years to catch up in all areas, but that it takes a good length of time for the concept to become accepted in everyday educational settings and thus for understandings to build from work from the 'shop floor'.

So, let's go back twenty years to a much quoted, pioneering paper by Joffe (1980). One of Joffe's statistics has been applied over-enthusiastically and without careful consideration of how it was obtained. This is the '61 per cent of dyslexics are retarded in arithmetic' and thus 39 per cent are not. Now it is not quite as simple as that. The sample for this statistic was quite small, some fifty dyslexic learners. The maths test on which the statistic was largely based was the British Abilities Scales Basic Arithmetic Test, which is just that, a test of arithmetic skills. Although the test was untimed, Joffe noted that the high attainment group would have done less well if speed was a consideration. The extrapolations from this paper would have to be cautious. Other writers seem to have overlooked Joffe's own cautious and detailed observations, for example, 'Computation was a slow and laborious process for a large proportion of the dyslexic sample.' I worked with a student who was identified as dyscalculic by the Butterworth screener (where two out of the five exercises focus on speed and accuracy in computation) but who went on to achieve a Grade A in GCSE maths.

I think there are two reasons why Joffe's paper is so frequently quoted. One is that it is a good paper and the other is that there are so few others from which to quote. Brian Butterworth is the UK's leading expert on dyscalculia. Sadly, at the moment Brian is often a lone pioneer. We need more researchers to follow Butterworth's initiative. There is some excellent work going on in Europe, much of it from Dehaene.

Definitions and labels

As a (lapsed) physicist I have a scientist's concept of what makes a definition. In physics one can control the variables and do pretty reliable experiments. People are difficult to control (especially as teenagers). In this respect I view some of the definitions used in the learning difficulty (LD) field as descriptions.

The definition of a learning difficulty can be very influential and can have many consequences. For example, it can influence the allocation of resources to an individual or to a school or to the education budget of an Education Authority. For an individual, knowing that your difficulties have a label may be a relief and a benefit, but it may also cause a reaction not at all dissimilar to that of grieving for a loss. So there needs to be a sense of responsibility and awareness of all these implications in those who create definitions.

There seems to have been a change in the culture of the definition of dyslexia, from the all encompassing definitions of the late 80s to the focused, minimalist definition of the British Psychological Society in the late 90s. This could well be significant. Professor Tim Miles talked of 'lumpers' and 'splitters'. So, could there be 'specific learning difficulties' that may encompass all or some of dyslexia, dyspraxia and dyscalculia or can the three 'dys's have independent existences? And does it matter if they don't?

Does being dyscalculic exclude you from being dyslexic or dyspraxic? Does being dyslexic exclude you from being dyscalculic? Then, turning to the lumpers, does being dyslexic mean you are also dyscalculic and dyspraxic?

It may help to answer some, if not all of these questions if you think of real people, real individuals and what the answer would be for Jeff or Jane. My feeling is that the answer to the first two questions is 'No' and to the third question, 'Not necessarily'.

Of course the answers depend on the definitions currently assigned to the difficulties. I'll come back to summarise my thoughts on definitions towards the end of this paper, but here is a small sample of definitions for now.

The first is from a DfES booklet (2001) on supporting pupils with dyslexia and dyscalculia in the NNS.

Dyscalculia is a condition that affects the ability to acquire mathematical skills. Dyscalculic learners may have difficulty understanding simple number concepts, lack an intuitive grasp of numbers, and have problems learning number facts and procedures. Even if they produce a correct answer or use a correct method, they may do so mechanically and without confidence.

Very little is known about the prevalence of dyscalculia, its causes, or treatment. Purely dyscalculic learners who have difficulties only with numbers will have cognitive and language abilities in the normal range, and may excel in non-mathematical subjects. It is more likely that difficulties with numeracy accompany the language difficulties of dyslexia.

The second dates from 1970 and is attributed to Kosc.

Developmental dyscalculia is a structural disorder of mathematical abilities which has its origin in a genetic or congenital disorder of those parts of the brain that are the direct anatomico-physiological substrate of the maturation of the mathematical abilities adequate to age, without a simultaneous disorder of general mental functions.

Sharma (1990) discusses three terms for difficulties in mathematics, saying that,

Terms such as acalculia, dyscalculia, anarithmetica . . . there is no definite agreement on their use universally in the literature . . . they have not been used consistently . . . although there are significant differences between dyscalculia and acalculia, some authors have used the terms interchangeably . . . the descriptions of these terms are quite diverse to say the least.

He explains dyscalculia and acalculia as:

Dyscalculia refers to a disorder in the ability to do or to learn mathematics, that is, difficulty in number conceptualisation, understanding number relationships and difficulty in learning algorithms and applying them. (It is an irregular impairment of ability.)

Acalculia is the loss of fundamental processes of quantity and magnitude estimation. (It is a complete loss of the ability to count.)

The final example is from a *DfES Consultation – Classification of SEN*, from descriptions to be used in the pupil-level annual schools census from 2004.

Specific learning difficulty (SpLD) covers a range of related conditions which occur across a continuum of severity. Pupils may have difficulties in reading, writing, spelling or manipulating numbers which are not typical of their general level of performance.

Pupils may have difficulty with short-term memory, with organisational skills, with hand-eye coordination and with orientation and directional awareness. Dyslexia, dyscalculia and dyspraxia fall under this umbrella.

Pupils with dyscalculia have difficulty with numbers and remembering mathematical facts as well as performing mathematical operations. Pupils may have difficulties with abstract concepts of time and direction, recalling schedules and sequences of events as well as difficulties with mathematical concepts, rules, formulas and basic addition, subtraction, multiplication and division of facts.

What distinguishes dyscalculia from just problems with maths? What do we mean by 'problems with maths'? How big is the problem?

We don't know, though the brain studies of Dehaene and Butterworth may take us there. It will depend on the definition. It may also depend on the perseverance of the difficulty. Goodness knows how many people have a 'difficulty' with maths. It is likely to be a significant percentage of the population, depending on which tabloid newspaper you read. Like all skills, if you cease to practise you lose the skill and few adults practise maths very often, especially topics such as fractions or algebra, after leaving school. So the extent of the problem could well increase in adults.

In an article from The Times *on 26 June 2006, 'Lacking in skills', the Confederation of British Industry is quoted as saying that, 'Business is still spending a small fortune on what is essentially remedial education. An utterly abysmal 17 million do not possess a grasp of numeracy that would be demanded of an 11 year old' (the population of the UK is 60 million, with a working population of 35 million).*

So I am sure that just having a difficulty with maths should not automatically earn you the label 'dyscalculic'.

Dyscalculia introduces another word into the vocabulary of special needs. Some see these words as labels and thus as descriptors of a person. That would not be helpful.

OK, I'm dyscalculic. So what?

I like the questions, 'What if?' and the follow up 'So what?' 'What if I am dyscalculic, so what?' I have to ask does being dyscalculic condemn the learner to being forever unsuccessful at maths. That then raises further questions:

What does it mean to be successful at maths? What skills and strengths does a learner need to be successful at maths? Is it important to be successful at maths?

At the school I founded and ran for nineteen years, a DfES-approved independent school for boys who were diagnosed as (severely) dyslexic, the results for GCSE maths were consistently significantly above the national average. Usually at least 75 per cent of grades were at C and above compared to the national average of around 50 per cent. Obviously I believe that if the teaching is appropriate then a learning difficulty does not necessarily mean lack of achievement. But, does a C grade or above in GCSE maths define success? That's a question for another article, so, for the purpose of this article let's assume it is one criterion and let's assume this is one piece of evidence that appropriate teaching can make a difference.

As for maths, well there is the maths you need for everyday life. This rarely includes algebra, fractions (other than $\frac{1}{4}$ and $\frac{1}{2}$), coordinates or indeed much of what is taught in secondary schools. It does include a lot of money, measurement, some time and the occasional percentage. Take, as an example of a real-life maths exercise, paying for a family meal in a restaurant: It needs estimation skills, possibly accurate addition skills, subtraction skills if using cash, and percentage skills for the tip.

The Russian psychologist, Krutetskii (1976), listed the components of mathematical ability which could act as a description of what a learner needs to be 'good at maths' and thus also act as a guide as to what may be the deficits that handicap the learner failing to be good at maths (see also earlier in this chapter).

1 An ability to formalise maths material (to abstract oneself from concrete numerical relationships).
2 An ability to generalise and abstract oneself from the irrelevant.
3 An ability to operate with numerals and other symbols.
4 An ability for sequential segmented logical reasoning.
5 An ability to shorten the reasoning process.
6 An ability to reverse a mental process.
7 Flexibility of thought.
8 A mathematical memory.
9 An ability for spatial concepts.

What is maths?

Could a person be good at some bits of maths and a failure at other bits? Do you have to fail at ALL bits to be dyscalculic?

In terms of subject content, early maths is mostly numbers. Later it becomes more varied with new topics introduced such as measure, algebra and spatial topics. Up to GCSE, despite the different headings, the major component remains as number. So the demands of maths can appear quite broad, and this can be very useful as some students may succeed in topics such as graphs, but number can be a disproportionate part of early learning experiences.

So, poor number skills could be a key factor in dyscalculia. This might suggest that we have to consider the match between the demands of the task and the skills of the learner.

In terms of approach, maths can be a written subject or a mental exercise. It can be formulaic or it can be intuitive. It can be learnt and communicated in either way, or combination of ways by the learner and it can be taught and communicated in either way or combination of ways by the teacher.

Maths can be concrete, but fairly quickly moves to the abstract and symbolic. It has many rules and a surprising number of inconsistencies.

In terms of judgement, feedback and appraisal, maths is quite unique as a school subject. Work is usually a blunt 'right' or 'wrong' and it has to be done quickly.

Even on this brief overview it is obvious that the demands of maths are varied. The importance placed on speed of working could also be another key issue for learners.

Attitude and the affective domain

I don't have the reference, but there was a study done in Scandinavia that summed up the influences of language and maths skills on life. Excuse me if I state the influences somewhat starkly. It is important to remember that people do not have to follow the conclusions of statistical analysis. Being good at English does not predict success in life. Being bad at English predicts failure. Being bad at maths does not predict failure. Being good at maths predicts success.

Of course we all know that being bad at maths holds no social stigma in UK and many Western cultures. Indeed it may well attract much mutual empathy. So the consequences of dyscalculia are going to have a better social acceptance than the consequences of dyslexia. (For example, I recently read a letter to *The Times* about a restaurant menu, complaining that since it had spelling mistakes the writer would not be eating there. That makes sense.)

Schools, of course rarely reflect life. In school there may well be significant consequences of being bad at maths, for example the allocation of the learner to a teaching group which may limit the levels of work in several other subjects. Also in school, unlike life, it's hard to avoid the stuff you don't like or the work you feel you can't do.

Two key factors that aid learning are ability and attitude. The latter can go a long way towards compensating for the former, but then the two factors are pretty closely interlinked, for example when success encourages good attitude.

Some learners just feel that they can't do maths. This may well be a consequence of early unsuccessful learning experiences or feedback that is seen as negative. The judgemental nature of maths, together with the culture of having to do maths quickly, can lead children to avoid the risk of being wrong again and again and thus to disassociate themselves from the learning experience (Chinn, 1995). Maths creates anxiety and, sadly, it usually seems to be an anxiety that does not facilitate learning. Ashcraft *et al.* (1998) have shown that anxiety in maths can have an impact on working memory and thus depress performance even more.

Some learners develop an attributional style for maths that makes their attitude personal, as in 'I'm too stupid to do maths', pervasive, as in, 'I can't do any maths' and permanent, as in, 'I'll never be able to do maths'. An individual with a combination of those three beliefs could well present as dyscalculic.

Memory, short, long and not always working

I often pose the question in my lectures 'What does the learner bring?' (to maths). I have already mentioned some factors such as anxiety. But what about memory? I know that Krutetskii (1976) lists mathematical memory as a requirement to be good at maths. I am sure that short-term and, especially, working memory are vital for mental arithmetic, particularly for those sequential, formula-based maths thinkers.

But can a learner compensate for difficulties in some of these requirements and thus 'succeed' in maths?

Now let's go back to school in England, where we had the National Numeracy Strategy. This truly was, in my opinion, a good programme in many respects, but however good the programme, it is virtually impossible to design a curriculum that meets the needs of every learner. An essential part of the NNS in the early years of education was mental arithmetic. Now that's an activity that needs memories, long, short and working. So a learner with a poor ability in any or all of short-term memory, working memory and long-term mathematical memory could fail at mental maths, even though he may have the potential to become an effective mathematician. If failure is internalised as a negative attributional style by the learner then that potential may never be realised.

Is Krutetskii's mathematical memory a parallel with Gardner's multiple intelligences? Perhaps there are multiple memories. That would explain some of the discrepancies I have seen in children's memory performances. Like any subject, there is a body of factual information for maths and if a learner can remember and recall this information then he will be greatly advantaged and if he can't . . .

So, good memories may be required for doing maths in general. Short-term and working memories may be essential for mental maths and mathematical long-term memory will be essential for the number facts and formulae you need when doing mental arithmetic.

Counting on and on

The first number test on the Butterworth dyscalculia screener is for subitising. This means an ability to look at a random cluster of dots and know how many are there, without counting. Most people do this at six plus or minus one.

A person who has to rely entirely on counting for addition and subtraction is severely handicapped in terms of speed and accuracy. Such a person is even more handicapped when trying to use counting for multiplication and division. Often their page is covered in endless tally marks and often they are just lined up, not grouped as ⵌ, that is, in fives. Maths is done in counting steps of one. If you show them patterns of dots or groups, they prefer them as lines and lines. If the learner is stuck at the counting in ones stage, then they will not develop a sense of numbers and the values they represent.

It's not just the ability to 'see' and use five. It's the ability to see nine as one less than ten, to see $6 + 5$ as $5 + 5 + 1$, to count on in twos, tens and fives, especially if the pattern is not the basic one of 10, 20, 30 . . . but 13, 23, 33, 43 . . .

It's the ability to go beyond counting in ones by seeing the patterns and relationships in numbers (Ashcroft and Chinn, 2003).

Garden variety or what?

How do we distinguish between a 'garden variety' poor reader and a dyslexic? (Stanovich, 1991) How do we distinguish between a 'garden variety' poor mathematician and a dyscalculic?

I think the answer has a lot to do with perseveration of the difficulty in the face of skilled and varied and appropriate intervention.

Can you be a good reader and still be a dyslexic? Can you be good at some areas of maths and still be dyscalculic? My guess is that the answer to both questions is 'Yes', but for maths it is partly because maths is made up of topics, some of which make quite different demands. And for both questions, good and appropriate teaching can make such a difference. The negative side reflects the developmental nature of maths and the dependence of many topics on work that has gone before.

Once again I drift back to problems with numbers as being at the core of dyscalculia. And it is numbers that will prevail in real life, when algebra is just a distant memory. And I guess that the main problem is in the belief of many adults that these facts can be accessed accurately and quickly, usually straight from memory, rather than via strategies.

Could there be a parallel between phonics and number facts? For example knowing how to use phonics to spell a word compared to using addition facts to add, say, 572 + 319.

But then not all factors are intellectual. A difficulty may be affected by a bureaucratic decision. Some bureaucrats specify a level of achievement that defines whether or not a child's learning difficulties may be addressed or even assessed, influenced in this decision, at least in part, by economic considerations. But, even then, is a child's dyslexia or dyscalculia defined solely by achievement scores? Is there room to consider the individual and what he brings to the situation? Sometimes these decisions are being de-personalised. So, I foresee a child not receiving provision for dyscalculia unless his maths age is five or more years behind the norm, which could mitigate against early intervention for six-year-old pupils.

Teaching

I claimed that being a physicist influenced the way I think. I am also a teacher and was for over forty years and those years have certainly influenced the way I think, too. The teacher part of my thinking says, among other things, 'So he's dyscalculic, what do you expect me to do next?'

Well, my guess is that using the range of methods and strategies we developed at the specialist schools I ran for teaching dyslexic pupils will also be effective with dyscalculic pupils. Indeed we probably taught many pupils who had the comorbid problems of dyslexia and dyscalculia. What we addressed as teachers was the way the pupil presented, not a pupil defined by some stereotypical attributes.

The key question, when faced with a learner who is struggling with learning maths, is, 'Where do I begin? How far back in maths do I go to start the intervention?' This may be a difference, should we need one, between the dyscalculic and the dyslexic who is also bad at maths. It may be that the starting point for the intervention is further back in the curriculum for the dyscalculic than for the dyslexic. It may be back to the earliest experiences, where counting was in ones and probably only forwards. It may be that fundamental concepts such as place value were never truly understood, merely articulated. Yet another topic to research. It may also be that the subsequent rates of progress are different. Another topic to research.

And for a final thought in this section, I ask, 'What is the influence of the style of curriculum?' I know, for example, from a European study in which I was involved (Chinn *et al.*, 2001), that the design of the maths curriculum certainly affects thinking style in maths.

So what?

Not being competent at maths may shut down many career options. There is some evidence that people who are good at maths earn more over their working life.

There are many reasons why a child or an adult may fail to learn maths skills and knowledge. For example, a child who finds symbols confusing may have been successful with mental arithmetic, but then finds written arithmetic very challenging. There may be other examples of an onset of failure at different times which will most likely depend on the match between the demands of the curriculum and the skills and deficits of the learner, for example, a dyslexic will probably find word problems especially difficult and a child who is not dyslexic, but is learning at the concrete level may find the abstract nature of algebra difficult. A child who is an holistic learner may start to fail in maths if his new teacher uses a sequential and formula-based 'inchworm' teaching style. A learner may have a poor mathematical memory and the demands on memory may suddenly exceed his capacity.

A difficulty will depend on the interaction between the demands of the task and the skills and attitudes of the learner. For example, if one of the demands of mental arithmetic is that it be done quickly, then any learner who retrieves and processes facts slowly will have learning difficulties. Learning difficulties are obviously dependent on the learning task.

And none of the underlying contributing factors I have discussed are truly independent. Anxiety, for example is a consequence of many influences. I am hypothesising that the factors I have mentioned are the key ones. There may well be others and the pattern and interactions will vary from individual to individual, but these are my choices for the difficulties at the core of dyscalculia.

Of the definitions of dyscalculia that I have quoted, I much prefer the one below. I have added some extra notes into the definition, which may then be better seen as a description (and thus not a label).

Dyscalculia is a perseverant condition that affects the ability to acquire mathematical skills despite appropriate instruction. Dyscalculic learners may have difficulty understanding simple number concepts (*such as place value and use of the four operations, $+$, $-$, $\times$ and $\div$*), lack an intuitive grasp of numbers (*including the value of numbers and understanding and using the interrelationship of numbers*), and have problems learning, retrieving and using quickly number facts (*for example multiplication tables*) and procedures (*for example long division*). Even if they produce a correct answer or use a correct method, they may do so mechanically and without confidence (*and have no way of knowing or checking that the answer is correct*).

This version focuses on number, which makes sense to me. It mentions memory and it includes those who present as competent in some areas, but whose performance has no underlying understanding of number. An addendum could list some of the key contributors, such as:

A learner's difficulties with maths may be exacerbated by anxiety, poor working memory, inability to use and understand symbols, and an inflexible learning style.

Now the definition/description is in this form, it may be possible to set up a diagnostic procedure, but it would have to be a very adaptable protocol.

Finally, have I met any learners whom I think would be described accurately as *perseverently and exclusively* dyscalculic? I have, but they were few. I mention two, one is a female, gifted in language (and languages) who had absolutely no idea what '$\frac{1}{2} \times 50$' (presented as symbols) would be. I asked her would the answer be bigger or smaller than 50 and she replied 'Yes'. The other is a male, average at language skills but who could not 'see' that I held out *three* fingers. He had to count them, even as a sixteen year old. He achieved a Grade G in GCSE maths. But, as for the number of students and adults with significant learning difficulties in maths, I suspect we are looking at over 20 per cent.

There are many others out there who may present as dyscalculic as young learners. It's what happens next that confirms or challenges that description.

References and further reading

Ashcraft, M.H., Kirk, E.P. and Hopko, D. (1998) 'On the cognitive consequences of mathematics anxiety' in Donlan, C. (ed.) *The Development of Mathematical Skills*, Hove: The Psychological Corporation.

Butterworth, B. (2003) *The Dyscalculia Screener*, London: NFER-Nelson.

Chinn, S.J. (1995) 'A pilot study to compare aspects of arithmetic skill', *Dyslexia Review*, 4, 4–7.

Chinn, S.J. and Ashcroft, J.R. (1992) in Miles, T.R. and Miles, E. (eds) *Dyslexia and Mathematics*, London: Routledge.

Chinn, S.J., McDonagh, D., Van Elswijk, R., Harmsen, H., Kay, J., McPhillips, T., Power, A. and Skidmore, L. (2001) 'Classroom studies into cognitive style in mathematics for pupils with dyslexia in special education in the Netherlands, Ireland and the UK', *British Journal of Special Education*, 28, no. 2, 80–5.

DfES (2001) *The National Numeracy Strategy. Guidance to support pupils with dyslexia and dyscalculia*, DfES 0512/2001.

Joffe, L. (1980) 'Dyslexia and attainment in school mathematics: Part 1', *Dyslexia Review*, 3, no. 1, 10–14.

Kosc, L. (1986) 'Dyscalculia', *Focus on Learning Problems in Mathematics* 8, nos 3–4.

Krutetskii, V.A. (1976) in Kilpatric, J. and Wirszup, I. (eds) *The Psychology of Mathematical Abilities in School Children*, Chicago: University of Chicago Press.

Seligman, M. (1998) *Learned Optimism*, New York: Pocket Books.

Sharma, M. (1990) 'Dyslexia, dyscalculia and some remedial perspectives for mathematics learning problems', *Math Notebook*, 8, nos 7–10.

Stanovich, K.E. (1991) 'The theoretical and practical consequences of discrepancy definitions of dyslexia', in Snowling, M. and Thomson, M. (eds) *Dyslexia: Integrating theory and practice*, London: Whurr.

For me, the main issue here is that not every child or adult who is failing in mathematics is dyscalculic. Even for those who do gain this label, it does not predict an outcome, but it does suggest to me that whatever teaching experiences this dyscalculic pupil has had, they have not been appropriate. I know, from ten years of data on pupils at my last school, that it is possible for most pupils to change a history of low gains in maths age, often fewer than six months per year, to gains of over twelve months per year, thus moving to 'catch up'. Some of these pupils might have been diagnosed as dyscalculic, some might not. In many senses that was less relevant than their history of underachievement in mathematics.

And would intervention for a dyscalculic be different? The answer is that any difficulty has to be viewed individually, but that the core principles of teaching and learning will probably be drawn from the same compendium of ideas used for dyslexics.[5]

Adjusting lessons to help pupils who are having difficulties in learning maths

Adjustments to lessons should be based on four principles:

1 *Empathetic classroom management*, which implies an active awareness and consequent adjustment to the learning strengths and difficulties of pupils.
2 *Responsive flexibility*, which allows the teacher to have a repertoire of resources and strategies which respond to the individual (and often changing) needs of the pupil.
3 *Developmental methods* are methods that address the remedial need while developing mathematical skills and concepts.
4 *Effective communication*, which infers an awareness of thinking and learning style and an awareness of limitations such as language skills, poor short-term memory or slower speeds of working.

The application of these principles should affect all levels of work, from the construction of the syllabus and lesson plans to the setting and marking of homework.

Integrating dyscalculic pupils and other learners who have difficulties with mathematics into the real world of the classroom

The syllabus and programme of work

1 A structure or programme that builds in regular returns to topics helps learners with poorer long-term memories. Frequent revisions and overviews, especially after a short time lapse for reflection help to reinforce learning. The explicit linking of numbers, operations and basic concepts.
2 Programmes that rely heavily on self tuition can allow pupils to develop incorrect procedures and concepts (I remember the Kent Mathematics Project, where pupils worked largely with work cards and at their own pace, but with little or no tuition). This will be true of many programmes that are exclusively IT based (see Hattie).

In the classroom

1 Short-term and working memory deficits can affect mental arithmetic skills (which may sometimes show a marked difference in success to written arithmetic skills).

2 Short-term and working memory deficits can affect many other areas of learning such as the number of items of instruction a pupil can recall and process at one time. These deficits may be auditory or visual or both, so presentation should always address both modes.

3 Look out for short-term memory overload (when the pupil will just be overwhelmed and recall nothing at all).

4 If recall of facts (such as times-table facts) and procedures (such as subtracting from zero) do not become not automatic, then there is less mental 'space' left to do the main task. This compounds the effect of difficulties. Select 'easy' numbers when introducing new arithmetical procedures.

5 Reading deficits do not affect all areas of mathematics to the same degree and are a good example of a deficit that gives rise to a seemingly inexplicable change in level of performance (for example, when word problems are introduced).

6 Some pupils are slower to produce work, due to such factors as writing speed, poor organisational skills, finger counting instead of instant recall of facts. Speed of working is often an issue in mathematics and can be the cause of greatly increased anxiety and greatly decreased levels of performance. Consider allowing extra time for tests and examinations. Consider careful selection of quantities of work set for these pupils.

7 Anxious learners are often poor risk takers and will not try work they perceive to be difficult, thereby avoiding failure (they have usually had enough experience of failure), but they are then not accessing new learning experiences. Research in the 1920s showed that a pupil's first experience of applying new knowledge is the experience that persists . . . a big problem if he gets that first experience wrong. Allow pupils to experiment and fail as one of the steps on the path to success, but this has to be a closely controlled strategy.

8 Some pupils are intuitive, answer-orientated problem solvers who may not learn from a step-by-step, sequentially orientated, formula dependent teacher, and, of course, vice versa. There are also significant implications for documentation of work. Intuitive workers are usually disinclined to document. These differences in thinking style (thinking through problems) are present in the whole school population, including teachers, but their affect on pupils with dyslexia, dyspraxia or dyscalculia (with their other contributing problems) is likely to be more critical (see Chapter 4).

9 Sequential, formula-orientated learners with poor memories are at risk of failure in mathematics.

10 Inaccurate intuitive, answer-orientated learners are at risk if they are inaccurate *and* if they do not learn to document their work.

11 Dyslexic pupils do not adjust quickly to changes in routine, for example if new teacher expects a different page layout in exercise books.

12 Accessing all the basic facts can be an issue for many children, so consider giving them a times-table square to stick into the back of their exercise book (so that they have to make some effort to turn to the information) and make sure they can track successfully to the answers.

13 Learning is usually more effective if it is presented in a multisensory way. This includes the use of concrete manipulatives, which are often phased out as being 'too young' for secondary pupils. Manipulatives may be used as demonstrations, using demonstrations of the materials or interactive whiteboards. This avoids the 'babyish' image when used by an older learner.

14 Money is an effective manipulative and is one step on to abstraction from a directly proportional manipulative such as base ten blocks. Also it is likely to be more acceptable for older learners.

Concrete materials and manipulatives

Please see Chapter 9 for a discussion of materials and manipulatives.

Books and worksheets

1 Worksheets and textbook layouts can be overwhelming, for example, by the use of lots of small print, closely spaced or by fussy, confused pages with cartoons and disjointed text. Try providing a cover sheet/window that reduces the quantity of material facing the pupil.

2 The reading level may be beyond the pupil. If a book cannot be replaced in these economically hard times either provide a photocopied 'translation' or make sure you or another pupil reads the problem to the pupil with difficulties. This is particularly relevant for coursework and investigations.

3 If a dyslexic pupil is having difficulty setting out work on the page, discuss giving them an exercise book that has bigger/smaller/squares.

Homework

1 Deal with the pupils who are forgetful and badly organised. Take a positive attitude and make sure they have the information and equipment they need. Parents of such pupils have usually suffered alongside their child as they struggle through school. You could try to liaise with them, for example by giving them a homework timetable. Remember, difficulties may be familial.

2 Give homework in a form that they can access. For example check the vocabulary. Make sure the homework is read to the pupil before they take it home. Get high-tech and provide a memory stick so that work can be done on computer – and that PC could even have the facility of voice output.

3 Consider allowing the pupil to use a calculator (with all the cautions I know many teachers have about their use) or a number square or a table square.

Marking

1 Mark new work before too many examples have been attempted. Do not let error patterns become ingrained.

2   Mark diagnostically. For example, the pupil may have used the correct procedure, but made an arithmetical error. Do not just mark work 'wrong'. Say how it was wrong and what can be done to put it right.
3   Remember the pupil who may work more slowly than his or her peers. Consider selecting fewer examples but still giving the breadth of experience.
4   Be encouraging.
5   Avoid red pens and big crosses and scribbles. (Try green and small and neat and, better still, constructive comments such as 'Small addition error here, rest OK'.)

Remember

Pupils are individuals. Some will need some of these suggestions, some will survive without any of them. However, I do not think that any learner will be disadvantaged by any of these suggestions and many will be advantaged. The suggestions may reduce some of the learning (special) needs in your classroom and even prevent the onset of some problems.

This book acknowledges that pupils are individuals. I have long had a suspicion of any scheme, intervention or cure that claims it is 'for all'. I suspect that the only part of this book that is 'for all' is the emphasis on understanding each pupil.

The catch-22 of catch up

If a pupil falls behind he or she will have been working more slowly than their peers. To catch up he or she will have to progress faster than their peers. It is possible.

2 Factors that affect learning

This chapter is about some of the factors that may contribute to a learner having difficulties with mathematics. Factors such as a poor working memory can have a considerable impact on many of the topics that make up mathematics.

At the end of the section on each factor I have left space for the reader to add his or her own suggestions. I could never claim to know all the solutions, especially as it is so important to remember that what works for one student may well not work for another. Hence, the need for a range of solutions, to be used in response to the (often labile) individual needs of each learner.

Quite often the 'Suggestions' section includes the advice to 'take time and evaluate'. The culture of doing maths quickly can be totally opposite to the correct approach of appraising before reacting, irrespective of the anxiety it can create (see Chapter 7).

Some suggestions address a problem right away while others may take longer. The impact depends on both the nature of the problem and the needs of the learner.

Schools and colleges should work towards building up a bank/library of appropriate resources, so that many of these problems can be addressed from materials that have been prepared before. This takes time, but can also be an opportunity for collaboration between staff.

Short-term memory (STM)

The problem	Suggestions
Some children will have weaker short-term memories than their peers. This may be a developmental lag or a persistent problem. What is relevant here, however, is the realisation that there will be a range of short-term memory capacities among the pupils in any classroom. Teachers should know which students have weak short-term memories. A STM for three items, for example, will have an extensive impact on absorbing information.	
This will have an impact on the pupil's ability just to keep up with the lesson in general.	Do not give lengthy strings of instructions. Imagine someone giving you a nine-digit phone number to remember by presenting it, once, spoken quickly and

The problem (cont.)	Suggestions (cont.)
	with no breakdown into chunks of numbers. So present 712563449 as 712 563 449 or 71 25 63 44 9 or whatever chunking size the learner can deal with.
In mental arithmetic it may be a challenge for them to remember the question.	Repeat the question, and/or put the key numbers on the board.
The procedure they are trying to use to solve the question may have too many steps for their short-term memory capacity to recall the original question.	Ask what method they are trying to use. If appropriate suggest an alternative method, or accept an estimate. Perhaps allow them to make memory jottings for intermediate steps (halfway house to full mental work).
When attempting mental arithmetic questions they are handicapped by slow retrieval of basic facts.	Provide a table square or a basic addition facts square.
	Give them questions that use the facts they do know (usually 2, 5, 10) so that you test the process not the basic facts.
When copying questions from a page, worksheet or a board they only copy one or two or three items (letters or numbers) at a time and may mix up parts of questions, creating new, extra questions.	Provide a worksheet that they can write on. Use colour or highlighters to help them to track their position on the board or worksheet.
	Mark the questions they create rather than the ones you gave.
Remember, the easy option is for the learners to opt out and not try the work.	Be aware of this attitude, which will build into a major self-esteem and attributional style issue.

Add your own suggestions and solutions (and extra problems!)

Working memory

The memory used for working things out 'in your head'. Obviously a prerequisite skill for mental arithmetic, but also helpful in written problems, for example, in that with an effective working memory you may not have to write as much. There is increasing evidence that a deficit in this skill has a major impact on learning and doing maths (see researchers such as Pickering, Gathercole and Packiam Alloway). As with short-term memory, teachers and tutors should know which students in their class have weak working memories.

The problem	*Suggestions*
Poor performance in mental arithmetic.	One has to ask why some educators and policy makers think that mental arithmetic is a 'good thing' for all students. If a student's working memory is weak (I recently assessed an art graduate in her mid-thirties, highly successful in her special field, who had a working memory for three items only . . . this is not a problem that children grow out of) then they will not succeed in mental arithmetic, unless there is appropriate differentiation.
	Select questions that do not overload working memory.
	Allow some learners to make notes.
	Have a basic fact square (multiplication and/or addition) available, so that time and memory capacity are not wasted on accessing facts.

Add your own suggestions and solutions (and extra problems!)

Long-term mathematics memory

This is long-term memory for mathematical information. It may be a specific memory and thus might be weaker than memory for other information.

The problem	*Suggestions*
Some pupils find that instant recall from memory of basic addition facts a persistent problem, particularly in exams.	Allow finger counting (but be aware that this will not develop number skills).
	Teach pupils how to build on key addition facts such as doubles or number bonds for 10. For more detail, see below.
	Teach pupils to write the number bonds for 10 as their key facts and teach how to derive other facts from these bonds.
	Teach pupils how to draw up an addition square (see Chapter 5).
Some pupils find that instant recall of multiplication facts is a persistent problem.	Give pupils a tables square (and show them how to use it . . . for division too).
	Teach pupils how to create their own multiplication facts square.
	Teach pupils strategies that build on the 'easy' facts. For example, double the 2× facts to obtain the 4× facts, or work out the 9× facts by working back from the 10× facts. For more detail see Chapter 5.
A pupil cannot remember the long multiplication algorithm.	Teach repeated addition (in chunks of 2×, 5×, 10×, 20×, etc.). See Chapter 5.
A pupil cannot remember the division procedure.	Teach repeated subtraction (in chunks of 2×, 5×, 10×, etc.). See Chapter 5.

Add your own suggestions and solutions (and extra problems!)

Direction

Some children find the directionality of maths a challenge. The problem will be greatly exacerbated by inconsistencies such as division (see below).

The problem	*Suggestions*
Some will find counting backwards problematic, more so than you, the teacher, might predict or realise.	This will require more practice, perhaps asking for smaller sequences of reverse order numbers, starting with 'one less, one back from *x*'.
	Start from different numbers. Try counting back in 2s, 5s, 10s (also as 76, 66, 56, 46 . . . as well as 70, 60, 50, 40 . . .). Then introduce 9s and relate to 10s.
	Try counting to a target number: 18, 16, 14, _, _, _, 6, 4.
	Point out patterns, using colour to highlight the pattern.
The pupil hears 'nineteen' and writes 91 (which actually follows the digit order of the word, as is the case for all the 'teen' numbers).	The teen numbers are the exceptional two-digit numbers, with the unit coming before the ten (teen) (see Transposals, p. 37).
They may find the change from positive coordinates to negative coordinates disproportionately more difficult.	A chance to remind learners to look for detail, to absorb before reacting.
	Perhaps the learner could label the axes negative and positive boldly and appropriately. Refer back to work on the number line. This may pre-empt the problem.
Children may also be phased by the change in direction of the steps for traditional short and long division compared to the right to left working for addition, subtraction and multiplication.	Teach alternative methods, for example, repeated addition or subtraction.
Confusion may arise over the different ways in which division is represented, for example 54 divided by 9 can be written as $54 \div 9$ or $9\overline{)54}$ or $\frac{54}{9}$.	Make sure you do not assume pupils will automatically take on board these representations. Explain the meaning alongside the alternatives.
	In the $\div$ symbol, the dots are replaced by the numbers of the fraction – that is, in this example the dots are replaced by 54 (on the top) and 9 (on the bottom).

The problem (cont.)	Suggestions (cont.)
The sequence of place values as you move left or right of the decimal point may confuse, especially when the language is considered, as in hundreds and hundredths.	Show the digits as you say the words.
	Use a visual image or concrete material such as base ten blocks. This is one ten*th*, one divided into ten equal parts, '$\frac{1}{10}$' or money with 10p as $\frac{1}{10}$ of £1. The relationship between $\frac{1}{10}$ and 10 can be considered with 10p and £10, bringing in language and rewording such as 'How many 10ps in £10?' compared to the abstract '10 divided by $\frac{1}{10}$' (which also rephrases a division question as a multiplication question).
	Point out the focus of the symmetry. It is the unit digit, not the decimal point.

Add your own suggestions and solutions (and extra problems!)

Visual

The problem	Suggestion
Think about the 'look' of a page, a worksheet, a test.	Look carefully at presentation when choosing textbooks or when designing a worksheet (see also Speed, p. 26). Try to 'Keep it simple'.
If the presentation is crowded, with little space between lines or questions, then some pupils will experience anxiety.	Illustrations may help the look of a page. They should be pertinent.
	If lines of print are set too close then pupils may mix up lines, taking some information from one line and some, incorrectly, from another line.
	Try providing the pupil with a piece of card with a window or slot cut into it so only a part of the page is revealed.

The problem (cont.)	Suggestions (cont.)
In an attempt to be more user-friendly some book designers have made the layout very fragmented.	Look for simple, clear design. Try the window strategy (see previous).
The symbols for the four operations can be confusing if not written or printed carefully. A + can be close to a ÷. A little rotation can make a + and a × indistinguishable.	Choose a clear font at a suitable size.
	Also be wary of learners perseverating – that is, continuing to add, for example when the problems have changed to subtract. The pressure of working quickly can exacerbate this problem, as can anxiety. Encourage the learner to relax and to subvocalise the symbols or highlight them.
Pupils may mix up questions, taking part from one line and part from the line below.	Line off questions or space them out.
	Try a coloured overlay. Black print on white paper blurs the images for some readers (Crossbow Education is a supplier of coloured overlays – see Appendix 2).
	Mark the question they have created rather than the one in the book!
The page seems blurred.	Try a coloured overlay. Try printing worksheets on coloured paper.
	Try different coloured print.
	Suggest a visit to a specialist behavioural optometrist (see the BABO website).
The pupil finds copying from the board a problem.	Provide a handout or use coloured pens to break up information. Keep presentation clear and well spaced out. Try not to talk when pupils are copying (some pupils cannot dual task – that is, listen and write at the same time).
Pupils cannot draw a 2D representation of a 3D figure, for example a cuboid.	Try providing isometric paper.
	Show how the drawing of a cuboid is made up of two off-set rectangles joined by parallel lines.

Add your own suggestions and solutions (and extra problems!)

Speed of working

In a recent large-scale survey by the author on maths anxiety, 'Having to do maths quickly' was ranked in the top six (of twenty) items that made students (male, female, mainstream and dyslexic students) anxious.

The problem	Suggestions
Teachers often expect learners to do mental arithmetic problems quickly.	Allow selected pupils to have a little more time. For example, ask the question, say you will come back to them, ask another learner (or two) and then return for the answer.
	Slow recall of basic facts may be the slowing influence. Give the pupil a table square or an addition square.
	Give part of the answer, for example, asking for 64 + 78, ask for the unit digit '64 plus 78 is one hundred and forty . . .' or structure 'What is 8 add 4? What is 60 add 70 add 10?'
Pupils may find homework (and class) tasks difficult to finish.	Set fewer questions, but ensure the pupil gets to experience the range, as in setting, say, the even number questions (thus revising that concept too). Provide worksheets where the pupils fill in gaps rather than writing out all of the question. Don't overface the learner.
Pupils take an impulsive approach to the maths problems.	For word problems, encourage them to read through a problem, rephrase it, draw it if possible. For number problems encourage them to verbalise it, for example for 85 − 17, subvocalise, '85 minus 17, 85 take away 17' using different phrasing (see Chapter 6).
Pupils are slow to start work at all. There could be several reasons . . . They did not hear all the instructions (poor short-term memory, inattention, distractions, hearing).	Repeat instructions, chunking them, not giving too many steps at once. Make sure he has heard by asking him (quietly and individually) to repeat the instructions. Use a buddy.
They are avoiding the work (anxiety, attribution, attitude).	The first two reasons need long-term nurture (see Chapter 8). Attitude could be due to several causes and needs, try using empathetic discussion.

The problem (cont.)	Suggestions (cont.)
Pupils fail to finish a test within the set time.	Provide them with a different coloured pen or pencil and allow them to carry on until they have tried as many of the items they feel can attempt.
They haven't got all the necessary equipment (book, pen, calculator).	If there is a support assistant, this could be part of their brief. Establish a routine.
	For example, have equipment ready to give out and have a system to make sure it is returned (mark it clearly!). (*More suggestions in 'No attempts'.*)

Add your own suggestions and solutions (and extra problems!)

No attempts

A sign that students are withdrawing from involvement in maths. An informal survey, by the author, of hundreds of teachers around the UK and around the world suggests that many pupils are starting to give up on maths at age seven (and sometimes younger).

The problem	Suggestions
A pupil leaves lots of unanswered questions.	Pupils who think they can't succeed at a question may decide to not try rather than get it wrong, so this is partly an anxiety/attitude problem. So check if they understand the topic and ask what it is that is making them not attempt the work. 'What is it you don't understand?' (Do not accept, 'Maths' as an answer! Ask them to be specific, this is a diagnostic question).
	Is there a pattern to the missed questions? (More diagnosis) Were they absent when that topic was taught?

28

The problem (cont.)	Suggestions (cont.)
A pupil is slow to start work.	It could be that the pupil is badly organised . . . can't find the book, pen, etc. If this is a regular occurrence, have a 'buddy' pupil pack for him/her.
	It could be that avoidance of failure is stopping the pupil. Try asking them to attempt just one or two questions (this has another very important benefit. If a pupil makes an error in his first practice of a new topic, that error pattern will establish itself, setting up the need for intensive remediation in the future).
	Try sitting the pupil at the back of the class so you can walk over to them and focus on them without the other pupils noticing it. This could be negotiated instead of sitting the pupil at the front where everyone sees the reminders.
	Allow the pupil to have a 'buddy' to tell him/her what to do.
A pupil has no idea how to begin.	Offer a starting hint or do the first line.
	Offer a model answer.
A pupil starts the exercise, but gives up after two or three questions.	This could be the 'quantum leap' effect. Some exercises and worksheets start with two or three relatively straightforward and easy questions and then, 'wham!' the next question is so very much harder that the pupil goes into the 'no attempt' strategy. Check the worksheet or exercise by actually doing the questions and imagining you are that pupil. Then modify the work.

Add your own suggestions and solutions (and extra problems!)

Recording/writing up

The problem	Suggestions
The pupil only writes an answer. There is no record of the method/procedure used.	This may be a consequence of a 'grasshopper' thinking style (see Chapter 4). Pupils should be encouraged to discuss their methods and be shown how to record their methods. This could be done by the teacher modelling the technique or providing an exemplar answer 'frame'.
The pupil writes very cursory notes.	This may be a consequence of slow writing skills rather than the pupil not knowing what to do. Allow more time and/or reduce the number of examples they are required to do. Provide a sheet with the key vocabulary. Give them notes.
Writing is extremely untidy and disorganised.	Try squared paper of variously sized squares until a suitable one is found.
	Offer a worksheet where the writing demands are minimised.
	Allow the pupil opportunities to talk through their methods so they can show their abilities.
Copying from the board. This requires the student to look up, focus on the board, find the correct place, remember some data, refocus on his paper/book, write the data in the correct space, refocus on the board and repeat the procedure. This is very influenced by short-term memory.	Offer notes. Allow the pupil to photocopy the notes from a student who produces good notes.
	If the material is in a textbook, allow the pupil to highlight key areas.
	Check regularly, that the pupil has, at least, adequate notes.
	Provide notes.

Add your own suggestions and solutions (and extra problems!)

Poor recall of basic facts

This is a particular example of a long-term memory problem. See also Chapters 3 and 5.

The problem	Suggestions
The pupil makes many basic fact errors, such as $7 + 6 = 12$ or $6 \times 7 = 67$ within 'longer' computations.	Have a supply of basic fact squares (expect losses).
	Supply a calculator, suggesting it is just used to access the basic facts rather than doing the whole calculation.
	Show how to make a 'number bonds for 10' chart: 10 9 8 7 6 **5** 4 3 2 1 0 0 1 2 3 4 **5** 6 7 8 9 10 (note the emphasis for 5, acting as a check) and show how to use it to obtain other facts.
Poor knowledge of basic factors handicaps factorising quadratic equations.	Teach some patterns to reduce the extent of the problem, such as looking for even numbers (2 and 4), fives and zeros (5), digits adding to nine (9), digits adding to three, six or nine (3).
	Provide a table square and revise how to use it for factors (division).
	Show how to fill in a blank table square.
	Make sure the early questions involve only simple factors, so the pupil can focus on learning the procedure.

Add your own suggestions and solutions (and extra problems!)

Poor reading skills (see also Chapter 6)

The problem	Suggestions
The pupil has difficulty in reading.	Check if the pupil needs spectacles or a better (and possibly bigger) print (many photocopiers can enlarge print). Try a coloured overlay to change the print/paper contrast (Crossbow Education is a supplier, see Appendix 2).
The pupil has difficulty in reading word problems (but understands them if they are read to him or her).	Read them to the pupil (though this takes your time and may damage their self-esteem if not done discretely and with empathy).
	Provide the pupil with a personal dictionary, with the necessary vocabulary for this topic – previously read, explained and discussed.
	Check the non-mathematical vocabulary (names, places, etc.). Change it to easily decodable alternatives, for example, Ocraville to Bath.
	Scan the work into a computer and let the pupil use voice output.
The pupil has difficulty in understanding/interpreting word problems.	Encourage the pupil to reword the question.
	Encourage the pupil to try and represent the problem as pictures.
	Try one of the reading acronyms, e.g. SQ3R . . . Survey, Question, Read, Review, Respond (if nothing else it counteracts impulsivity).
	Give number sentences and encourage learners to create word problems for themselves (see Chapter 6).

Add your own suggestions and solutions (and extra problems!)

Sequencing skills

The problem	Suggestions
Pupils have difficulty remembering and recalling sequential information.	Point out and demonstrate the pattern.
	Don't wait too long for the learner to discover the sequence for themselves.
Number sequence for 2 beyond 10.	Start with the part they can recall 2, 4, 6, 8 ('Who do we appreciate?') and use it as a base, pointing out the patterns **12**, **14**, **16**, **18** . . . **22**, **24**, **26**, **28** . . . possibly using coins or base ten blocks. This can also be a task where the learner progresses from counting on in ones. The difference between consecutive numbers is two each time.
Number sequences for 10 when the unit digit is not zero. The pupil can recall 10, 20, 30, 40 . . . but finds sequences such as 13, 23, 33 . . . challenging.	A good chance to enhance place value concepts. Again use coins or base ten blocks to show the pattern. This time the units digit is the stable factor. The difference between consecutive numbers is ten each time.
	Use a 1 to 100 number square and point out/colour in the 'plus 10' patterns.
	Use a 100 bead string.
General number sequences.	Encourage the pupil to work out the differences between consecutive numbers and thus know if the difference is always the same or if the differences create a new sequence (finding the 'bridge' between numbers).
	For sequences such as adding (or subtracting) 6, 7, 8 or 9 each time suggest that the addition or subtraction be done using the easy numbers. So, to add 6, add as 5 and 1 or to subtract 9 take away 10 and add back 1.
Incorrect decimal sequence as . . . 0.7, 0.9, 0.9, **0.10**.	Use 10p coins alongside the written numbers, that is, write the decimal and place the coins, write the next decimal and add another coin.
	Discuss where the 0.1, 0.2, . . . sequence is heading. It is heading for 1.0.
	Offer a sequence with gaps . . . 0.1, 0.2, __, 0.4, __, __, 0.7, 0.8, __, __, 1.1, __, 1.3.

The problem (cont.)	Suggestions (cont.)
Incorrect fraction sequence as . . . $\frac{1}{10}$, $\frac{1}{11}$, $\frac{1}{12}$ where the learner assumes that $\frac{1}{12}$ is the biggest of the three fractions.	Go back to the fractions that are (should be) known – that is, half, quarter and third, and place these in order of size.
	Demonstrate with folded paper. Discuss sharing slices of cake and pizza, but remember that these are not true (precise) fractions. Use a clock (time) for halves and quarters. Establish the concept that fractions involve division.
	Remind them that fractions cannot be taken at face value. Learners have to look beyond the numbers that they see or write and remember the hidden division sign.
Procedural sequences/algorithms (e.g. long division).	Try to support memory with understanding.
	Find an alternative procedure that relates to the pupil's thinking style (see Chapter 4).
	Find a mnemonic (e.g. BODMAS) but do not use the mnemonic strategy too often less the mnemonics themselves become another burden on mathematical memory.
Pupils have difficulty entering data into a calculator in the correct sequence as in 'Take 16 from 47' or $7\overline{)542}$.	Encourage the pupil to be wary, not rush and write the problem in symbols then appraise and compare the original question and its symbolic form.
Pupils have difficulty continuing a sequence if it does not start at the beginning, as in 'What is the next number after 6?' The learner goes back to '1, 2, 3, 4, 5, 6 . . . 7'.	Show the whole sequence, for example with wood or plastic numbers, then take away some of the beginning numbers and/or some of the end numbers.
	Show how to identify the interval (gap) between consecutive numbers in the sequence.
	Say a series of numbers and ask the pupil to join in at different points.
	Show parts of sequences, for example, 46, 48, 50, 52 . . . or 34, 39, 44, 39, 54 . . . and ask pupils to identify the sequence.
	Model the sequence with a bead string, base ten materials, Cuisenaire rods.

Add your own suggestions and solutions (and extra problems!)

Transfer of skills

The problem	Suggestions
The pupil can only add when the numbers are presented in the simple standard vertical format.	Practise the skill in a 'problem' context, working from the digits to language, 'Add 41 and 38' to more complex language . . . in small steps.
The pupil can combine 2×8 with 5×8, but cannot combine $2y + 5y$.	Demonstrate/model the transition with, say, number rods.

Add your own suggestions and solutions (and extra problems!)

The 'terminal' (extreme) inchworm/grasshopper (see Chapter 4)

The problem	Suggestions
The pupil will only respond to and work in one thinking mode. His thinking style is fixed at one end of the continuum.	If, after much empathetic intervention, the learner's thinking style remains inflexible, then you, the teacher will have to work with that situation. This will mean accepting the learner as they are and giving them the appropriate instruction for their restricted thinking style. One consequence may well be that they have to learn how to identify questions that are unchangeably grasshopper and not waste time trying to answer them. This is pragmatism at a level that will sit uncomfortably with many teachers, but it may be the kindest (and most effective) way of teaching these rareish pupils.

Add your own suggestions and solutions (and extra problems!)

Order

The problem	Suggestions
The learner hears 'Ten past seven' and writes 10:7.	Time is one of those topics that is so familiar in everyday use that we may forget the problems it generates. The learner should be taught to repeat the time putting in hours and minutes, 'Ten minutes past seven hours' and know that the written convention is 'Hours: minutes'.
The learner reads 'Take 8 away from 18' and writes 8 − 18.	The learner must be taught to be wary of even the most innocent looking word problems and rephrase them until they make sense. The fact that 8 − 18 either looks impossible or leads to a negative answer should suggest caution.
In an addition sum such as 56 + 37, the learner adds 6 and 7 to make 13, writes down 1 and carries 3.	The teen numbers are misleading in that the unit syllable comes before the tens syllable. (See Chapter 6.)
	This may also be down to lack of automaticity. Using a fact that is 'known' in isolation does not mean it can be accurately recalled when used in a computation.

Add your own suggestions and solutions (and extra problems!)

Not checking an answer

The problem	Suggestions
The learner checks (often quickly and inadequately).	Try to encourage checking by an alternative method. This helps to encourage flexible thinking styles (see Chapter 4).
	Try to encourage a check via an estimate. Ask 'Does the answer make sense?' (You may have to explain what you mean by 'sense').
	Use the basic estimate question, 'Is the answer bigger or smaller?' (adjusted to make contextual sense).
The learner doesn't check at all.	Ask what rough value (for numeracy) the learner expected for the answer. Allow a wide guess/estimate and edge them towards closer estimates. This could be part of the training towards risk taking.

Add your own suggestions and solutions (and extra problems!)

Organisation

The problem	Suggestions
The pupil always arrives at lessons without key equipment.	Suggest the pupil obtains a pencil case or similar holder in which to keep just the essentials (list the 'essentials').
	Be prepared to lend equipment, but be even more prepared to remember to collect it back at the end of the lesson (the pupil will forget). Make sure the equipment you lend is clearly marked!
The pupil's written work on the page is badly organised.	Try squared paper, offering different sizes of square to find what suits.
	Try vertical lines.
	Try modelling good layout. Provide a scaffold.
	Try a worksheet where part of the work is written.

Add your own suggestions and solutions (and extra problems!)

Transposals

The problem	Suggestions
The pupil transposes numbers, for example, writing 31 for thirteen. This is likely to be the consequence of the words we use for the 'teen' numbers. These are the only two digit numbers where the units digit is named first, as in *four*teen.	Try place value cards (Figure 2.1) or coins to model the correct digit order (check if transposals only occur for teen numbers, where the words do mislead, as in thirteen . . . three ten, rather than twenty-three, which does not).
	Explain the language structure of a teen number compared to the digit structure.
	Explain that the teen numbers are exceptional and to be wary when they are around. Show how transposals can be a problem when adding numbers such as 27 + 36 becoming 81 instead of 63 since 7 + 6 is added as 31. Encourage the learner to evaluate such answers by estimates.
	Play card search games, with cards that show, for example, 16 and 61 and ask for 'sixteen' or 'sixty-one'.

Add your own suggestions and solutions (and extra problems!)

Generalisations and recognising patterns

The problem	Suggestions
The learner does not recognise patterns. Some lessons rely on pupils making the discovery of a pattern. This may not always be a reliable method (for example, a pupil may process in groups of three and the pattern may be in groups of four).	Be more overt in hinting at the pattern. Use colours. Use materials (use trial and error to find the match between learner and material). For example, base ten blocks may work as an illustration of multiplying and dividing by ten (a deceptively tricky task), possibly in conjunction with a place value sheet.

Add your own suggestions and solutions (and extra problems!)

Language and symbols

Please see Chapter 6 for details on this topic.

Task analysis

In order to be pre-emptive, it may be worth doing a task analysis for a new topic. This can be a quick procedure, just thinking about the topic and making notes on the sheet below. The analysis can consider the topic, of course, but it can also take into consideration the nature of the learner(s). For example if the group contains a number of students with vocabulary and/or language problems then you might give more thought to that particular aspect of the task. A task analysis can be useful in focusing attention on areas where some pre-emptive action may greatly reduce the number of learners developing a problem with the topic and/or reduce the intensity of the problems.

Analysing from the prerequisite subskills perspective (Chapter 4) may also help a tutor/teacher understand where learning may falter.

TOPIC		
Factor	Problem	Suggestion
Vocabulary and symbols		
Language		
Short-term memory		
Long-term memory		
Sequences		
Direction		
Organisation/ spatial		
Thinking style		

Figure 2.2 A blank task analysis form

TOPIC	Mental addition of two-digit plus two-digit numbers	
Factor	Problem	Suggestion
Vocabulary and symbols	A variety of words imply +	Vary the vocabulary of the questions. 'What is 46 *add* 72?' '43 *plus* 56?' 'What is the *total* of 61 and 39?'
Language	Should not be an issue with mental addition, unless wrapped up in a complicated story.	
Short-term memory	May not remember the question. May not have enough short-term memory to do the question.	Repeat the question. Try an alternative method. Ask a part question.
Long-term memory	The usual problem of recall of basic facts, and possibly of 'carrying'.	Use sums with known facts, e.g. 74 + 75, so doubles can be used.
Sequences	Not a main problem in this topic, but the answer may well be computed in the reverse order, e.g. 74 + 75 done as 9 then 14.	Encourage pre-estimates and allow time for this or ask in two stages, that is first ask for an estimate and then the accurate answer.
Direction	Since 64 + 56 = 56 + 64 this should not be a problem, but see 'sequences'.	
Organisation/ spatial	Should not be a factor in mental work, but spatial memory may be needed.	
Thinking style	The pupil may use a method that is less suitable for his learning problems.	Encourage alternative strategies. Ask the pupil to evaluate and interrelate the numbers, e.g. 8 and 9 can be rounded up to 10.

Figure 2.3 An example of a task analysis

3   What the curriculum asks pupils to do and where difficulties may occur

This chapter in the first edition of *The Trouble with Maths* was based on the National Numeracy Strategy. Maths education in the UK moves on, but the content of the NNS was never that dissimilar to maths curricula from years gone by. In fact maths is likely to follow the same development of different strands and topics in many maths schemes across the world. Maths curricula are international and the difficulties in learning maths are international.

What I have done in this second edition is to highlight a range of key maths topics, look at the pertinent issues, predict where difficulties and confusions will arise and outline some possible solutions. Some of these are dealt with in more detail in other chapters, but to avoid the need to flick between pages, I have kept the content of this chapter somewhat self-contained.

This is the preventative medicine approach. Whatever the curriculum, the analogy I like is to compare preparing a maths lesson to preparing an expedition. You prepare for all the many problems that you know you are going to encounter, and experience helps you to predict what they will be, but then that experience also tells you that there will still be some problems you will not have predicted, but the trick is to be ready for them anyway. The curriculum is the basic outline for the journey. This chapter is the guide to some of the unpredicted events that may prevent your learners from having a successful expedition.

Place value

Place value is a basic, fundamentally important topic that sets the foundations for success in numeracy. A deep understanding of place value is essential for many future topics in maths. It should not be assumed that pupils will generate these links by osmosis. Many of the links will need explicit teaching. Also, it is easy to assume that an ability for recalling memorised information means that that information is therefore understood.

Most of the work in this topic area is within the pupils' previous experiences, the experiences that pre-date school. This is both a positive and negative influence. It is positive in the sense that pupils are working from familiar facts and awareness and should feel comfortable and confident, but negative in that they may already have formed some incorrect ideas and perceptions or maybe feel that because the work is familiar they do not need to consolidate and interrelate their existing fact base to new work.

> They come to formal education with a range of prior knowledge, skills, beliefs and concepts that significantly influence what they notice about the environment and how they organize and interpret it. This, in turn, affects their abilities to remember, reason, solve problems and acquire new knowledge.
>
> (US National Research Council)[1]

Place value is a key concept. Children who fail to grasp the idea of place value find numeracy difficult and in later stages of maths will make errors such as:

$$
\begin{array}{r} 45 \\ +88 \\ \hline 12\ 13 \end{array}
\qquad
\begin{array}{r} 45 \\ +88 \\ \hline 123 \end{array}
\qquad
\begin{array}{r} 45 \\ \times 22 \\ \hline 90 \\ 90 \\ \hline 180 \end{array}
\qquad
\begin{array}{r} 4\ \ 5\ \ \\ 10\overline{)4050} \end{array}
$$

These errors are serious in that they are rooted in a misunderstanding of this fundamental and influential concept. Such errors are a clear indication of the need to track back to the very basics of maths as your starting point for intervention. (Recognising errors is diagnostic. Marking answers wrong without that diagnosis is judgemental.)

Misconceptions about place value can arise from early experiences. For example, we introduce numbers as 1, 2, 3, 4, 5 . . . where the sequence 'gets bigger' as we track to the right. When place value arises, as with, say 24, the number to the left is 'bigger' (exacerbated by the previous experience of 4 being 'bigger' than 2). Such inconsistencies in maths can derail an insecure learner. Their prior experiences and knowledge from outside school may add to the confusion. If the Hindu-Arabic system of number that emphasises place value is to be understood, with all its mathematical implications, then it should be taught thoroughly, with images to support the concept (see Chapter 5). We may forget how sophisticated this concept is and how recently, relatively, it came to Western cultures. I looked at the plaque on an old bridge in Bath. It was built in MDCCCLXXXVIII. Roman numerals are not easy to work with! (It was built in 1888.)

Addition and subtraction, especially involving crossing the tens, hundreds, etc., will also be handicapped by a poor understanding of place value. Crossing the decades is part of place value and becomes an essential part of addition and subtraction. Equally multiplication by the both the traditional methods and the 'chunking' methods requires that place values are understood, so that, for example when multiplying by 45 the pupil needs to know and understand that the 4 is 40 and what affect this has on the multiplication. Pupils need to be able to break down numbers and that involves understanding place value. (Breaking down numbers can include using number relationships as well as place value, for example 50 as 100 ÷ 2 or 99 as 100 − 1 or 40 as 4 × 10.)

Manipulatives (see Chapter 9) can be helpful, particularly base ten blocks and coins that can give a visual image to the symbolic representations of numbers and the base ten system. Numbers that involve zero (such as 1004) often need extra explanation and again base ten materials may help. Try working from 1444, through 1044 to 1004 using the base ten blocks. Multiplying and dividing by 10 and powers of 10 may also help to show how the position of a digit in a number affects its value. My work on standardising the screener test for *More Trouble with Maths* revealed how poorly this aspect of the base ten concept, particularly dividing by 100, 1000 and so on, is understood and carried out.

Estimation and rounding and place value

Try work on placing a number in the correct position on number lines, both empty and full number lines. Work on rounding and linking estimation to accurate computations leads pupils to learn the skills of overviewing and checking problems. Estimation is an holistic skill and should be taught to complement the procedural skills of written arithmetic, even though pupils may show a marked preference towards just one of these skills (see Chapter 4). Remember that estimation is not precise, and is not meant to be precise, and that the required level of 'accuracy' of the estimation depends on the particular real-life situation. The 'empty' number line is a good visual for practising this skill.

There is a concern that students do not evaluate their answers. The definition of dyscalculia used in the UK (2001) notes that, 'Even if they produce a correct answer or use a correct method, they may do so mechanically and without confidence'. A survey of 391 special education professionals in the USA[2] identifying characteristic behaviours of students with teacher-identified maths weaknesses puts 'reaches "unreasonable" answers' ninth out of thirty-three.

Rounding is a strategy that strengthens the skill of estimation in the sense of 'levels' by rounding to the nearest ten, nearest hundred, nearest thousand. It is also a good real-life skill, particularly useful for shopping. (Why is it, that after all the maths education delivered across the world, shops still price items as £4.95 or £7.99 or £999 and many shoppers persist in interpreting these as £4 and £7 and significantly under £1000?)

Negative numbers

Negative numbers are really quite challenging to learners' everyday experiences. Many learners find counting backwards in positive numbers problematic, so counting back in negative numbers is going to be a big challenge to consistency. So it is good to use some real-life examples to explain the concept. Temperature and lifts ('going up' and 'going down') are real-life examples where negative numbers occur. Both these examples are a vertical representation of a number line and thus not the familiar horizontal form. Consistency is challenged again, but awareness helps!

So, the quite sophisticated sequence on a number line is:

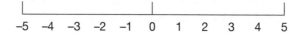

$$-5 \quad -4 \quad -3 \quad -2 \quad -1 \quad 0 \quad 1 \quad 2 \quad 3 \quad 4 \quad 5$$

This sequence takes the counting backwards skill beyond the zero. The rules of the positive number sequence are now reversed. In positive numbers, 4 is bigger than 3. In negative numbers, -4 is smaller than -3. In the first experiences of negative numbers these seeming inconsistencies can confuse uncertain learners and will need clear and explicit teaching. Consistency in the interpretation of number sequences is challenged again (and will be yet again with fractions).

Introductory work on adding to a negative number ($-3°C$, warming *up* by 4°C or starting 3 floors below ground and taking the lift *up* 4 floors) and subtracting from a negative number ($-3°C$ and cooling *down* by a further 3°C to $-6°C$) sets the foundation to work from an image that is 'real' to an abstract and symbolic representation ($-3 + 4 = 1$ and $-3 - 3 = -6$). This topic also revisits the idea that addition and subtraction are opposite versions of the same idea. The vertical number line may help illustrate the concept and the processes and act as an intermediate stage to the horizontal version. The vertical number line also gives meaning to *up* and *down*. (On a cold day, say $-8°C$, if I could take away $-9°C$, then the temperature would be $+1°C$. Minus a minus makes a positive change.)

Calculations and computations

Rapid recall of addition and subtraction facts

There will be some pupils for whom the task of recall of the so-called 'basic' facts will be difficult. The additional pressure of having to respond quickly will exacerbate their problem. It will be vital for these pupils and helpful for the others if the connections and patterns are explained. This has been an issue for many years. It seems that low achievers in maths rely on counting, rather than recall and linking facts. The use of non-counting strategies is far more prevalent in high achievers. If these strategies are performed quickly teachers may interpret these processes as retrieval.

One of the great pluses of maths is that facts can be linked. This is much less evident in other subjects. For example, if I know that the capital city of France is Paris, it does not help me know the name of the capital city of Bulgaria. If I know that $5 + 5 = 10$ then I can work out many things, for example that 5 per cent is half of 10 per cent or that $5 + 6 = 11$.

How People Learn identifies three key findings for learning. The second of these principles is:

> To develop competence in an area of inquiry, students must (a) have a deep foundation of factual knowledge, (b) understand facts and ideas in the context of a conceptual framework, and (c) organize knowledge in ways that facilitate retrieval and application.[3]

This is apposite at so many levels for students with difficulties in learning maths. The parts (b) and (c) support (a) for these pupils especially. For this population a key question is what constitutes 'a deep foundation of factual knowledge' and does this only infer straight retrieval from long-term memory?

However, even pupils with poor memories for basic facts will need to learn some facts in order to use strategies and make links. The question is, 'Which are the most useful facts?' For addition and subtraction these facts are likely to be the doubles and the number bonds for 10. The most useful facts are, not surprisingly, the ones that can be extended and used to access as many other facts as is possible.

The interrelationships of numbers will help students to build strategies that not only help them retrieve more facts, but will support their understanding of basic number and operation concepts. In terms of teaching strategies to students, it is important to realise that all pupils will benefit from learning these links. This is truly inclusive teaching. It is the low achieving students that tend not to develop strategies for themselves. They need guidance. The more able students may not extract all the generalisations and benefits for understanding concepts beyond addition and subtraction, so guidance may help them, too.

The key number bonds for 10 can be extended to the two digit equivalents such as $40 + 60 = 100$ and then to $62 + 38 = 100$. This involves understanding place value, although it can extend and support existing levels of understanding.

This progression may require a good visual image, probably based on base ten materials or money. A pattern can once more be used.

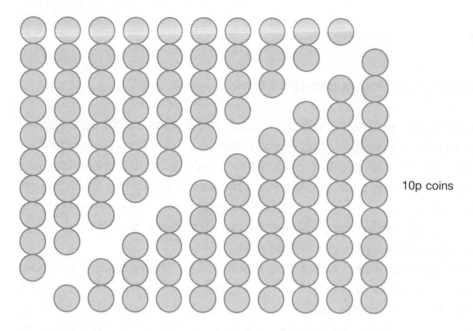

10p coins

Figure 3.1 Using 10p coins as images of number bonds for 100

The extension could be to a more complex pairing such as 62 + 38.

The 62 + 38 could be seen as in two parts, tens digits that add to 90 (done with nine 10p coins) and unit numbers (using ten 1p coins) that add to 10. The two groups of coins add to 100p, £1.

A second extension is to 1000, as with 850 + 150, which can be seen as two hundreds digits that add to 900 and two tens digits that add to 100. Another example of place value at work.

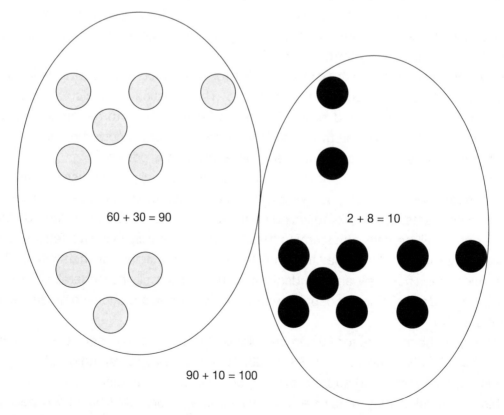

60 + 30 = 90

2 + 8 = 10

90 + 10 = 100

Figure 3.2 Coins to show 62 + 38

Extension of the doubles is a strategy used by many pupils and can be taught and organised to be consistent. For example doubles plus one may be used in 7 + 8 as (7 + 7) + 1 and the doubles minus one may be used in the same example 7 + 8 as (8 + 8) − 1. This also links to addition of even and odd, odd and odd and even and even numbers.

The key number bonds for 10 can be extended to the decimal equivalents starting with the decimal number bonds for 1.0 such as 0.2 + 0.8. A common error in retrieving these facts is in counting in tenths where the sequence is given as . . . 0.7, 0.8, 0.9, **0.10** (zero point ten) and for the previous example, 0.2 + 0.8 = 0.10. This extension of known facts may avoid that error. A further example of place value at work.

Extension to examples such as 6.2 + 3.8 (decimal number bonds for 10) follow the same pattern as for 100 and 1000.

The visual image for these decimal skills could be money. Pound coins represent whole numbers. So, for example, tenths can be represented by trading a £1 coin for ten 10p coins. These can be divided into two lots, demonstrating the number bonds for 10 extended to number bonds for 1 with the pattern written on the board, maybe using 0.50 + 0.50 as a key reference fact:

```
O  O     O  O
   O         O
O  O     O  O
```

A second level of splitting up the £1 is then shown by taking one 10p coin and trading it for ten 1p coins (these 'tradings' are reinforcing the concept of breaking down units into tenths and hundredths), so that there are now nine 10p coins and ten 1p coins, making £1. The two lots of coins can now be split, first the nine 10s then the ten 1s and the process used to demonstrate examples such as

0.62 + 0.38 = 1.00 = 1.0 = 1

Finally, the ten 1p coins can be used to demonstrate examples such as

0.07 + 0.03 = 0.10 = 0.1

There has to be a note of caution here. Earlier we used a 10p coin to represent 10 and a 1p coin to represent 1. This change (inconsistency) has to be explained before embarking on the demonstration.

This section provides good opportunities to build on and extend from key basic facts and thus help pupils understand the interrelationships of numbers and place value, which is an essential skill for mental arithmetic. It should also improve number sense by linking and relating numbers and number facts instead of seeing them in isolation.

The addition square

The same demonstration can be used for both the addition and the multiplication facts in order to illustrate progress through the task and the effectiveness of learning key facts and interrelating them to new facts. The starting challenge is 121 facts on the squares, which reduces as the easy facts and links are mastered. A square can be shaded in to show progress:

Facts learned	*Number of facts left to learn*
The whole square. Starting off.	121
adding on zero (0)	100
adding on 1 and 2 (finger counting)	64
adding on 10 (place value pattern)	49
adding on 9 (add on 10, subtract 1)	36
number bonds for 10	31
number bonds for 10 +/− 1	21
doubles	16
doubles +/− 1	10
What is left?	
5 + 3 and 3 + 5 (which relate to 4 + 4)	
7 + 5 and 5 + 7 (which relate to 6 + 6)	
8 + 6 and 6 + 8 (which relate to 7 + 7)	
8 + 4 and 4 + 8 (8 + 2 + 2)	
8 + 5 and 5 + 8 (8 + 2 + 3)	

Understanding addition and subtraction

It seems that for many learners that addition is the default operation. If all else fails, add. Subtraction is often avoided or the procedures/algorithms are only partially remembered and/or inaccurately carried out.

Vocabulary and language are often good places to start, since these are the obvious essentials for communicating with learners. The vocabulary of addition and subtraction is quite varied with, for example, 'more', 'plus', 'and', 'in all', 'altogether' and 'increase' are all used to infer +. Later on, in word problems, devious examiners and worksheet writers may well devise word problems where, for example, 'more' may mean subtract. There is a further comprehension factor in that some phrases have other meanings outside numeracy, for example, 'take away'. Thus the vocabulary is both varied and unreliable! (See also Chapter 6.)

Addition is the next step from counting on in ones. Subtraction is the next step from counting back in ones. If these counting skills are not secure, and that will include crossing the tens, then addition and subtraction may not be understood.

Many adults, and children, consider subtraction to be 'harder' than addition. The roots of this opinion probably lie in the emphasis given to the procedures/algorithms used when subtraction was taught at school (in my day it was 'borrow and payback', later it was 'regrouping') when it was understanding the procedure and its relationship to addition that was needed. Somehow the early experiences some children have of 'taking away' never result in understanding, generalisation and the link to addition.

These topics can be built on an understanding of the two operations and *their inter-relationship.* The links between the two should be mutually supportive. If addition is easier than subtraction that may be down to the fact that we practise counting up far more than we practise counting down. We could address this initially by working from the strength and teach how to subtract by counting on.

Materials, such as base ten blocks could be used to demonstrate counting back and crossing the tens.

Pupils can be shown how to be flexible with numbers, for example by using the commutative law (7 + 93 = 93 + 7) and the associative law (17 + 8 = 17 + 3 + 5 or 15 + 2 + 8). They can learn the link between addition and subtraction (8 + 7 = 15 and 15 − 8 = 7) so that these facts are connected in their learning experiences. Many supportive strategies depend on these links. The principle is to use the relationships between facts to aid learning, for example, 2 + 6 is more efficiently counted as 6 + 2 and that 'bridging' through 10 helps as in 8 + 7 is also 8 + 2 + 5 or 7 + 3 + 5. As above, there is the further link with 8 + 7, a link to the doubles 8 + 8 and 7 + 7.

In some curricula and in some maths programmes there has been an inclination to master addition first then tackle subtraction, but this may not link these two operations in the mind of the learner. Addition and subtraction need to be seen as mutually inverse procedures if flexible approaches to mental arithmetic and to checking answers to written problems are to be developed later. For example, as shown above, subtraction can be done and/or checked by adding on and crossing the tens.

Mental calculation strategies for addition and subtraction

These skills build on the previous section and rely very much on those prerequisite skills and facts being securely fixed in the pupils' memory. . . and retrievable from memory or by strategy . . . quickly (once again the expectation of speed of response may create additional anxieties in some learners and this in turn may have a negative impact on working memory. On the positive side, automaticity in accessing these facts will leave more working memory to deal with the problem). There is no doubt that a weak working memory will have a disastrous effect on the capacity to perform mental arithmetic calculations. It could be claimed that mental arithmetic discriminates against children with learning disabilities since working memory is frequently a problem in this population. Teachers need to know which of their students have poor working memories.

As well as being able to access basic facts, pupils should be aware of and use the relationship between addition and subtraction. Some simple demonstrations with the number line, moving forward for addition and backwards for subtraction and then discussing the significance of the difference between two numbers and alternative subtraction procedures such as counting on, emphasising the stepwise nature of this through, for example 10s and 100s (crossing the tens, etc.) may help.

An example is 1000 − 648, where 648 is the start point . . .

648 + **2** = 650 . . . 650 + **50** = 700 . . . 700 + **300** = 1000 . . . answer 352

Each of those steps uses the number bonds for 10.

Working on numbers near to tens is another useful extension of key basic facts into mental arithmetic, for example, the use of 10 for 9, 20 for 19, 100 for 98 and other similar examples. The procedure of adding 19 by adding 20 and subtracting 1 uses the inverse link of addition and subtraction as does the subtraction of 19 by minus 20 plus 1. Base ten blocks and/or money could be used to show the equivalence of adding, for example, nine 1p coins one at a time against adding a 10p coin then taking away one 1p coin.

Although this mental arithmetic skill is relatively easy to learn, the most likely confusion is that the pupil will do the wrong adjustment, so in 19 + 78, after adding 20 they might add 1 instead of subtracting 1. This is an indication that number values and relationships are not well understood. The question at the intermediate step, 'Is the answer bigger, smaller or the same (than adding 20)?' is useful yet again as a first estimate and check. A second check is from knowing that 9 + 8 gives a unit digit of 7. Learning checking strategies is essential for accurate mental arithmetic.

Much can be done by using the interrelationships between numbers to make mental arithmetic more accessible to more pupils. Pupils will benefit from looking at the numbers *before* selecting a method rather than reacting solely to the operation symbol. This is another situation where over-viewing is a good technique and another example of the negative effect of demanding speedy reactions. However, some pupils will only be secure if they have one, universally applicable method, so adopting this preliminary overview will not be a natural behaviour.

Mental arithmetic sessions have to be handled empathetically if some students are not to continually fail and then develop a sense of learned helplessness and withdrawal from these questions.

Written addition (and subtraction) is traditionally done from right to left, from unit digits to tens digits, hundreds digits and so on. If this method is transferred to mental addition, then the digits in the answer are generated in reverse order, that is the unit digit is calculated first, but stated last in the digits that make up the answer. If pupils add from left to right, starting with the highest place values first, then they can repeat the digits of the answer as they construct the answer, in the correct order. For example, adding 57 and 67 could start at 50 + 60 = 110, then 7 + 7 = 14, taking the answer to 124. The strategy of performing mental arithmetic 'in your head' by using the written algorithm/procedure demands a strong working memory.

So, it is likely that there will be a need to encourage and develop appropriate flexibility in approaches for addition and subtraction, not least to recognise that this will happen anyway as there will be different cognitive styles within the pupils in any class (see Chapter 4).

Paper and pencil procedures for addition and subtraction

These topics could be used to reinforce mental arithmetic methods by encouraging pupils to document procedures other than just the traditional algorithm (procedure). There will be some pupils who compute so rapidly and intuitively that documentation will not be easy for them. A classroom ethos which encourages different methods will help. On the other hand, there will be pupils who will be confused by exposure to too many alternatives ... the teacher's knowledge of an individual pupil's learning styles will enable him or her to balance and manage this. The question 'How did you do that?' usually diagnoses the method used. Another contributor to the classroom ethos is that of risk-taking.

There is significant evidence, from at least two major studies, one in New Zealand (Hattie)[4] and one in the USA (the National Research Council),[5] that meta-cognition, that is, understanding how you think, has a significant, positive impact on learning.

'Carrying, decomposition, renaming, regrouping, trading' all refer to an essential procedure. These processes which involve crossing the tens, hundreds, thousands, etc., boundaries are a development on from counting in ones and require an understanding of place value.

Crossing up, say from units to tens and crossing back, from tens to units are complementary and should be demonstrated together in order to reinforce the understanding of these particular processes. If subtraction and addition are perceived of as being opposite versions of the same procedure, then these two contributors to the operations of addition and subtraction are also equal opposites.

Of course, crossing the boundaries happened when counting in ones. Now the addition and the subtraction can be in numbers that are greater than one. However, the principle is the same and if the learner is not secure in their understanding of the principle when counting forwards and backwards, they do not have this necessary prerequisite skill for the next stage of arithmetic.

The relationship between addition and subtraction can be demonstrated with coins or base ten blocks. I prefer coins for older age groups as they have some reality and the trading that happens when the place value boundaries are crossed makes everyday sense. So, set up an addition with coins alongside the written numbers, say 57 + 78. Add the 1p coins to obtain 15p. Trade ten 1p coins for one 10p coin and carry it across to the tens column. Now add five 10p coins to seven 10p coins and add in the carried 10p coin to make thirteen 10p coins. Trade ten 10p coins for one pound coin (100) and 'carry' it to the hundreds column . . . answer 135. Make sure that each step with the coins is recorded as numbers written on paper.

Now reverse the procedure and subtract 78 from 135, which will require trading in the £1 coin for ten 10p coins and trading a 10p coin for ten 1p coins . . . renaming the 100 + 30 + 5 to 100 + 20 + 15. Do some other examples to support understanding and generalising. It is worth demonstrating and discussing each step first rather than the whole procedure. This should show the relationship between crossing the tens boundaries up and down.

Understanding multiplication and division

The four operations, +, −, × and ÷ are closely inter-related. A clear understanding of each operation and how it relates to the others will strengthen the understanding of the other operations. Multiplication is often described as 'repeated addition' but the understanding of this phrase may not be clear (it should be 'repeated addition of the same number' to be clearer). Similarly, division can be described as 'repeated subtraction'. *Students will need some concrete material experiences to start to develop these concepts. As ever, the symbols should be used alongside the manipulatives and visuals used for demonstration and discussion* (see also Chapter 9).

For example, to illustrate 6 × 7, six Cuisenaire rods, value 7, could be introduced, one at a time as 7 + 7 + 7 + 7 + 7 + 7 is written. The six rods could then be placed together to make a rectangle, giving an introduction to an area model for multiplication. There are, as ever, language considerations as well. The array is 'six lots of seven' and 'six times seven'. This can then be reversed to demonstrate division as repeated subtraction showing that 42 ÷ 7 gives as an answer of 6, the dimensions of the other side of the rectangle.

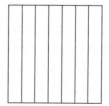

Figure 3.3 Cuisenaire rods for 6 × 7

The basic ideas in this section of work are the commutative property of multiplication (8 × 7 = 7 × 8), the distributive law [23 × 45 = (20 + 3) × 45 = (20 × 45) + (3 × 45)], the non-commutative nature of division and that division is the inverse of multiplication.

The connection between addition and multiplication can be explained by starting with times-table facts (see Chapter 5). Whenever possible, a new concept should be introduced and demonstrated with number facts that are automatic for the students.

Area is a good visual aid that can also help developing the skill of estimating answers. This can be presented with rectangles drawn on paper, squared or plain and base ten blocks (see also p. 54 in this chapter).

Multiplying by zero and by 1

Two simple concepts are introduced in this section. They may not have been taught in enough detail because they appear deceptively simple.

Multiplying by 1 does not change the value of a number (also useful to remember this when renaming fractions). Language could be a factor here. 'One lot of seven' is understandable whereas 'One times seven' is less so, unless you know the maths vocabulary, 'times'. This particular operation has been a significant stumbling block for many of the participants who took part in the standardisation of my basic fact tests. The confusion may be partly due to the fact that we rarely multiply by one in everyday maths.

Multiplying by zero results in zero. Many children believe there is a number somewhere, so big that it over-rules this law. Zero causes many errors! It's a place value concept, so it's back to basics to address this problem.

'Remainders'

The concept of a remainder is useful. There is a possibility that children may otherwise think that division always results in a whole number answer. It also raises a difference between multiplication facts and division facts. Learners may be asked, 'How many fives in fifteen?' which is a division fact directly related to a basic multiplication fact. The question, 'How many fives in sixteen?' is not a division fact. It is close to a division fact, but the answer now is, 'Three, remainder one.' I am less keen on the phrase, 'Three and *one left over*' since some children may be confused by the meaning of the '*three*' (fives) and the '*one*' which is 'left over'. This is another example where materials would help to clarify the meaning.

Rapid recall of multiplication and division facts (see also Chapter 5)

I have been asking teachers at my lectures and seminars, 'What percentage of 11 or 12-year-old pupils do not know all the times-table facts?' The answer is becomingly increasingly large, with some teachers saying 80 per cent.

Then there is the word 'rapid'. I can understand that 'rapid recall' may be of benefit when doing mental arithmetic. If these facts can be retrieved quickly with automaticity then there will be more working memory capacity left to do any calculation. However, the expectation of rapid recall will create anxiety in many students. In turn that anxiety may depress working memory capacity. In my 2009 survey of maths anxiety, 'having to do maths quickly' was one of the top ranked items for creating anxiety in secondary age students. This situation will probably generate reduced motivation and put a significant number of pupils into the 20 per cent who fail to reach the required standards in maths (a percentage that has not changed for decades). It seems unproductive to let this happen, since an inability to learn these facts does not preclude success as a mathematician. It might have an effect on a pupil's success in school, especially if maths is taught with this as a firm belief. Your classroom management of this objective will have a profound effect on your examination statistics.

An over-emphasis on rote learning of the times tables, even with the powerful 'self-voice echo' technique that I researched with Dr Colin Lane (www.self-voice.com) in the 1980s and an avoidance of the complementary division facts should be avoided.

Even and odd numbers

This may seem to be a low challenge topic, but there are other lessons to learn, as ever. Even numbers end (that is, have a units digit) in 0, 2, 4, 6 or 8. Every other digit in a number can be odd, it's that last one that matters, for example, 975,31**2** is an even number.

Any even number is exactly divisible by 2.

Odd numbers end in 1, 3, 5, 7 or 9. Every other digit in the number can be even, it's the last one that matters, for example, 864,20**7** is odd.

When odd numbers are divided by 2 there is a remainder of 1.

The rules for adding odd and even numbers can act as a low stress (partial) check on the answers to basic addition facts, for example, 7 (odd) plus 8 (even) should give an odd number answer.

Establish (or re-establish) the main idea that even numbers are about 2, about being exactly divisible by 2, using this as an early exposure to the concept of division, sharing into equal parts. And establish that an even number plus 1 makes an odd number. This can be demonstrated with Stern materials or Numicon, visual images that can lead into discussions of the concept.

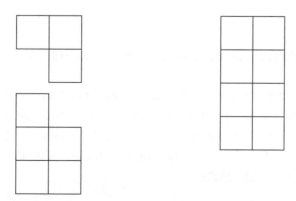

Figure 3.4 Numicon/Stern materials: odd plus odd = even

'Chunks'

One of the useful strategies that pupils may adopt is the breaking down of numbers into easier chunks. For example, doubling 72 might be difficult in one 'bite', but twice 60 plus twice 12 may be easier for some. 60 + 12 is a more creative split than the place value split of 70 + 2. The same is true when halving. Half of 60 plus half of 12 as 30 + 6 may be easier than half of 70 plus half of 2. Chunks can encourage flexibility, instead of always splitting according to place value.

Again, for example, half of 920 might look daunting, but half of 800 plus half of 120 may be easier for some. 800 + 120 is a more creative split than the place value split of 900 + 20. These decisions require a good sense of number.

Many pupils read numbers literally and in an upwards sequence. For example '9 is 9', the number after 8 rather than 1 less than 10. 25 is only seen as a number in the twenties, not as $\frac{1}{4}$ of 100 or $\frac{1}{2}$ of 50 or even as 20 + 5. 98 is seen as nine tens and eight units and not as 2 less than 100. Can your pupils learn to find the easy number breakdown? This is a very useful mental arithmetic skill, especially in life where so many prices use nines as the final digit in a number (139.9p per litre for petrol, £12.95 for a meal in a restaurant, £399 for a laptop). As ever, visual images will help many pupils. For example a 100 number line may help pupils see the closeness of numbers in the nineties to 100. Coins could also be used. One hundred 1p coins, organised into a pattern of rows of ten, show the closeness of, say 98 to 100.[6]

Fractions, decimals and percentages, ratio and proportion (see also Chapter 10)

Interrelating these three ways of representing numbers less than one (and bigger of course) will reinforce the understanding of each format. Keep referring to the common equivalents using them to provide 'markers' and illustrate other examples:

$\frac{1}{2}$ = 0.5 = 50%

$\frac{1}{4}$ = 0.25 = 25%

$\frac{1}{10}$ = 0.1 = 10%

$\frac{3}{4}$ = 0.75 = 75%

Using decimal notation for tenths and hundredths

Pupils will be familiar with money written as £3.49. This can be used to give an image of $\frac{1}{10}$, 0.1 and $\frac{1}{100}$, 0.01. Base ten blocks can be used to provide a proportional model. If pupils are having difficulty, show each decimal with money and base ten blocks. Add on coins or blocks, 0.1 and 0.01 to make new numbers. Discuss the place value, as base ten, coins and symbols (digits).

There can be a language and order/direction confusion here for some pupils. Whole numbers progress from right to left as units, tens, hundreds, getting bigger, while decimals go left to right as tenths and hundredths, getting smaller and with only a slight change in the sound of the words.

The symmetry in decimal numbers is around the unit digit and not about the decimal point.

Rounding a number with one or two decimal places to the nearest integer

The similarity of this process to whole number rounding should be explained. The use of shop prices such as £9.99 can be discussed as can the values of decimal numbers.

Relating fractions to their decimal representation

Focus on the key values of $\frac{1}{2}$ and 0.5 (It may help some pupils to discuss 0.5 and 0.50 – another directional difference with whole numbers, 0.5 and 0.50 are the same value whereas 5 and 50 are not and 05 is rarely used though it is used sometimes on forms for months, 05 is May, or in 24 hour timetables) and $\frac{1}{4}$ and 0.25, $\frac{1}{10}$ and 0.1, $\frac{1}{100}$ and 0.01. Set up a table and start to fill in some gaps, such as 0.2, which is $\frac{1}{5}$ (not $\frac{1}{20}$). Show how decimals can be combined, such as 0.3 and 0.5 to make 0.8 and compare this, without calculations, to combining fractions such as $\frac{3}{10}$ and $\frac{1}{2}$. Calculations for fractions to decimals can be shown with a calculator, especially if patterns are demonstrated ($\frac{100}{2} = 50$, $\frac{10}{2} = 5$, $\frac{1}{2} = 0.5$ and $\frac{100}{10} = 10$, $\frac{10}{10} = 1$ and $\frac{1}{10} = 0.1$).

Understanding percentages

Percentages are the third way of representing numbers between 0 and 1 (and bigger than 1 as pupils often do not realise that 200% is 2×). Work from 100% as 1, through 50% as $\frac{1}{2}$ and 0.50, 25% as $\frac{1}{4}$ and 25%, 10% as $\frac{1}{10}$ and 0.10 to 1% being $\frac{1}{100}$ of something (some pupils may need a brief revision of dividing by 10 and 100). If students can understand that 1% is $\frac{1}{100}$ and that it is obtained by dividing by 100 and that 2% is obtained by multiplying the 1% value by 2, that 3% is by multiplying by 3, that 4%, etc., then they have the foundation for calculating percentages by formula. Calculating 'easy' percentages is a further use for the skill of interrelating numbers. Fill in the gaps on a number line for percentages using 'easy' values by discussion such as where will 50% and 20% go? What fraction and decimal is it equivalent to? Is it twice 10%? Is 5% half of 10%? Do some simple calculations on '25% of' by halving 50% and do 5% calculations by halving 10%. Combine 25% and 50% to make 75% and 5% and 10% to make 15%. A 100 square is good for visualising percentage values.

Pencil and paper procedures (× and ÷)

Approximations for TU × TU are helped by reviewing the area model for multiplication. Some examples are given below.

31 × 17 can be seen, as a first estimation, to be over 300, just by counting the hundred squares. A second look would suggest an answer closer to 600.

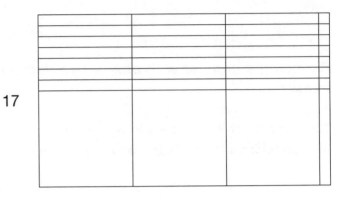

17

31

Figure 3.5 Area model for 31 × 17

28 × 39 can be seen in comparison to 30 × 40, giving an estimate of less than 1200.

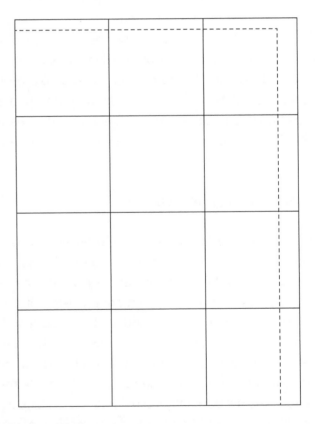

Figure 3.6 28 × 39 compared to 30 × 40 as areas

The area model also acts as a good illustration of partition methods. It also emphasises the units, tens and hundreds.

The long multiplication procedure is likely to be one of the first procedural barriers for pupils. It can be abstract so memory has less chance of a 'realistic hook' to hang from and the organisation of the various written stages, including the 'carried' numbers is challenging. The area model, shown in base ten blocks, or on squared paper or just as sketched rectangles shows where each part of the calculation originates. The area model is also valuable in fractions and algebra. This means the pupils are getting a consistent and developmental image. If you start with the area and one side, division leads to finding the value of the other side. So, the same image works for multiplication and division and shows the inverse relationship between these two operations.

Division by repeated (chunked) subtraction is the inverse of multiplication by adding chunks (partial products). It can also be shown on the area model.

I like the partial products created when setting up key multiplication values, that is $1\times$, $2\times$, $5\times$, $10\times$, $20\times$, $50\times$, $100\times$ and so on, using a pattern. So, for example, to divide 1537 by 18, set up the table, using the patterns:

$$1 \times 18 = 18$$
$$2 \times 18 = 36$$
$$5 \times 18 = 90$$
$$10 \times 18 = 180$$
$$20 \times 18 = 360$$
$$50 \times 18 = 900$$
$$100 \times 18 = 1800$$

The answer to $1537 \div 18$ can be seen to lie between 50 and 100, closer to 100. Subtraction of multiples will take the pupil to an answer.

1537	
−900	50×18
637	
−360	20×28
277	
−180	10×18
97	
−90	5×18
7	Answer: 85 remainder 7

This does relate to the standard written method. Both are by step-by-step subtraction of multiples of (in this case) 18.

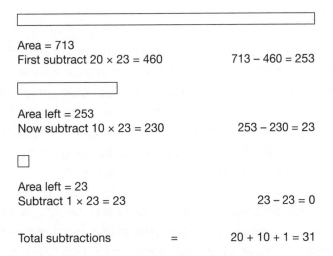

Area = 713
First subtract $20 \times 23 = 460$ $713 - 460 = 253$

Area left = 253
Now subtract $10 \times 23 = 230$ $253 - 230 = 23$

Area left = 23
Subtract $1 \times 23 = 23$ $23 - 23 = 0$

Total subtractions   = $20 + 10 + 1 = 31$

Figure 3.7 Division by subtraction of 'chunks'

Checking the results of calculations

One way of checking the addition of a column of numbers is to identify the combinations that make 10. For example look at the units column:

$$
\begin{array}{r}
46 \\
31 \\
87 \\
44 \\
33 \\
89 \\
+78 \\
\hline
\end{array}
$$

There are '10 combinations' in the units column, 6 + 4, 1 + 9, 7 + 3. With the unmatched 8, this makes a total of 38 (using this procedure also revisits and thus practices the number bonds for 10). Some pupils may introduce more sophisticated number combinations, such as 8 + 7 + 5 = 20.

Another method of adding down a column of numbers is to use tallies. This method helps pupils with poorer short-term memories. So, with the example above, as you add down the units column, 6 + 1 = 7, 7 + 7 = 14. Put a stroke through the 7 to mark the ten from the 14 and just move on with 4. So 4 + 4 = 8, 8 + 3 = 11. Put a stroke through the 3 to note the ten from the 11 and move on down with the 1 unit. 1 + 9 = 10. Put a stroke through the 9 to mark another ten. 0 is added to 8, 8 goes in the units place of the answer column. There are three 'ten tallies', so 30 carries over to the tens column as 3 tens.

Checking calculations is usually most effective when a different method is used for the check. Pupils who have flexible approaches to procedures are likely to be much better at checking and evaluating their answers. Flexible thinking styles are explained in Chapter 4.

Solving problems

Making decisions

Some problems could be presented where the pupils are not actually required to work out the answer. For example, they could be asked to estimate an answer. This could be as basic as 'Is it bigger?' or 'Is it smaller?'. Pupils could be asked which operation they would use, +, −, × or ÷, and to explain how. This could also lead to useful discussions and comparisons of methods. (The vocabulary around the four operations is varied in content and interpretation. The English language provides several ways of inferring add, subtract, multiply and divide – see Chapter 6.)

Making up 'number stories' is an important activity. Too often teachers expect pupils to 'translate' word problems into mathematical equations/statements while forgetting the reverse translation. By doing this pupils can learn how word problems are constructed (usually resulting in a totally boring, anorak questions in textbooks) and how misleading features can be introduced, such as extraneous data. It can also be fun and creative!

Making up number stories can help pupils understand how key words can be used to mean different operations and move them away from an overly literal interpretation of vocabulary (again, see Chapter 6).

Reasoning and generalising about numbers or shapes

It is not always easy for pupils to explain their reasoning for a mental calculation. It will help this objective if the classroom ethos is open and flexible. Even then some pupils may find that their method is so intuitive (and quick) that they cannot really explain all that happened in the brain. This may improve as pupils become accustomed to the idea of analysing their thinking.

Of course, once a teacher knows the procedure used by a pupil, she or he might be tempted to suggest changes or alternatives. This may not always be the best move and instant change may well not be possible for the pupil. This whole area of meta-cognition is fascinating and important. Ideally pupils should learn to be flexible in their choice of methods, being able to use successfully a range of procedures and discuss what they are doing and why. For most pupils this will happen over a period of time of exposure to the idea and encouragement to work in this more open manner. It must not be assumed that pupils can adjust their thinking style overnight. (For more details on thinking style see Chapter 4.)

This topic area can be used to develop further flexibility in using numbers and to show the interrelationships, especially those which make the manipulation of numbers easier, for example 49×30 calculated via 50×30. Again the language and vocabulary is pertinent, in this case '49 times 30' compared to '49 lots of 30'.

Spatial examples can be a break from number crunching activities and may well allow some pupils who have strong spatial skills to succeed.

Unstructured questions of the type $t + h + w = 1$ *will confuse some pupils. Some will just not have the confidence or skill to actually start the process, even with encouragement. Be prepared to lead more than you might want!*

Angle work enters a new world where a key value is 90, not 100 and where the length of the two lines which meet to make an angle do not effect the size/value of the angle.

There are ample examples of angles around us in everyday life that can be used to set the scene for this section. Again it is possible to build on what the pupil knows, but may not have internalised or related. Right angles abound and it is easy to show aspects of two, three and four right angles. A clock face is a good source for 360°, 30°, 90°, 180°, 270° and so on. Diagonals across a square show 45°.

Problems involving 'real life', money and measures

A maths programme should provide ample opportunity for reviews, revisits and revision. Over-learning is a strong, constructive factor in the acquisition of numeracy skills. Additionally, the interlinking of different sections can be used to help develop and consolidate concepts.

Presenting concepts and facts in a 'problem' format, that is, as a word problems possibly with real-life content, should be an exercise in developing understanding of concepts and developing problem solving skills.

Teachers can use these topics to introduce some truly 'real-life' work, such as money, exchange rates and measures. It would seem an ideal section in which to use manipulative materials such as coins, bottles, scales and such. Let pupils experience 100g, 100ml and see everyday recognisable examples to give them a basis for judging their answers in this area.

For foreign exchange it would be good to have some foreign currency, and possibly discuss which values of coins and notes are chosen and why (for example, the UK works on 1, 2, 5, 10, 20, 50, 100, etc.).

When dealing with recipes, talk about the reality of proportions when calculations may lead to $5\frac{1}{2}$ eggs. Perhaps do some costing for recipes.

With questions on time, remind pupils that 60 and 12 are the key numbers. Practise counting through a minute and an hour (58 seconds, 59 seconds, 60 seconds, which is also 1 minute. 58 minutes, 59 minutes, 60 minutes, which is also 1 hour).

There can be some conceptual problems with the 24-hour clock. It is not the familiar base ten. The two most likely confusions are with 20:00 hours (8pm) and 22:00 hours (10pm), so try to pre-empt the difficulty. The clock is now the only base 12 experience we have.

Handling data

Some students who struggle with numbers can experience success in these topics. It is worth including some topics when this is the case in any intervention programme. It's not much fun to always face work that you find difficult.

Probability

This is a topic that lends itself to discussion around events which are within a learner's experience and from which the mathematical groundwork can be naturally derived. Probability is 'everyday', covering topics such as the chance that it will rain to the probability of it being an *Eastenders* night.

It allows involvement of all pupils and is an area of maths which, in the introductory stage, is not a matter of producing an exact answer to be correct. In this introductory stage, pupils can get a feel of probability values (and perhaps a more rational understanding of risks that are often overstated). As ever, it allows for some cross linking to other topics. For example, an understanding of fractions may be improved when considering probabilities such as $\frac{1}{50}$ compared to $\frac{1}{10}$.

Organising and interpreting data

Collecting and classifying data is usually a less stressful and less judgemental activity. With careful instruction most pupils should produce acceptable work in this area. The word 'frequency' may cause some confusion and needs a good and clear definition.

There is computer software that prints out charts, giving an opportunity to discuss the clarity and appropriateness of presentation. This can also circumvent the drawing problems some pupils may exhibit (for example, dyspraxic pupils). Alternatively, pupils could be given support by supplying a partially completed graph, say with the axes already drawn and labelled, or a data sheet with the chart already drawn and ready for the pupil to use for collecting data.

There are sets of data that can be collected that allow the involvement of all pupils, for example, the colours of cars or vans passing by the school, the heights of pupils, shoe sizes, dates of birth (the day or the month), particular words in a newspaper, comics/magazines, popular sweets and so on.

For line graphs pupils need to know the significance of starting an axis at a value other than zero (and how this can distort the relative values of data . . . a qualitative link to proportion). The labelling of axes is another habit that pupils need to acquire.

This section also acts as an early experience of averages as a 'central' measure and an opportunity to evaluate data objectively. This should again give enough opportunities for realistic inclusion.

Measures, shape and space

The shape and space section could reveal a new group of pupils who have strengths in these topics in maths and another group that find these topics and concepts more difficult.

Measures

This section allows ample scope to work on pupils' existing experiences and bring together experiences to create understandings and concepts. For example, pupils know the standard soft drink can size and can be shown that this is close to $\frac{1}{3}$ of a litre. This fraction can then be shown in terms of cl and ml. The contents of a drinks can can be measured exactly and the result used for discussion on averages and the place of 'precise' and 'approximate' measurements in everyday life. The new work can be built around everyday experience and previous numeracy knowledge, combining revision and awareness in order to develop understanding.

Basic relative values, such as 10mm = 1cm, 100cm = 1m, 1000mm = 1m and 1000m = 1km need to be experienced with 'real-life' examples as well as memorised.

The metric prefixes of m, c, d and k are not always perceived to be consistent. It is a shame that m can be used for metre, milli, mile and minute. The kilogram is an anomaly as a standard unit compared to the metre and the litre. Also, the kilometre is often viewed as a separate unit to the metre, since the scale and use of this unit is not necessarily connected to the relatively small-scale, classroom-sized metre. The development of an appreciation of the size of the quantities represented by these units may well need to be addressed explicitly. It is both important and extremely useful to know that the metric prefixes are consistent. (I do feel that examiners and writers of exercise/textbooks sometimes inadvertently exacerbate this problem by setting deliberately confusing questions.)

The confusions that might arise in this section can be reduced by using the ample opportunities available to show real items that relate the theory to experience and give learners a baseline, reference image for measures.

Reading from scales is an important, cross-curriculum skill and estimating a reading that falls between divisions is a good estimation skill that relates back to numbers and the number system and the empty number line. Using a large scale (that is with big distances between divisions) could help. Circular and curved scales should also be demonstrated. This also offers some revision of proportion.

Areas may need a fundamental revision before moving to the new work. It always impresses me that 7×7 is an area very close to half of 10×10. Area requires new estimation skills. This shift in comparison parameters is demanding and may well be helped by building up some 'easy' areas with unifix cubes or similar. It can also be used to discuss square numbers. Areas can also be used to show the link between multiplication and division.

Perimeter and area can be confused during calculations, so it is helpful to establish a clear picture in students' minds for each word. A simple image link such as perimeter *fence* (fence suggests a line) may suffice. It is also useful to emphasise the units used and to create a visual image of a square centimetre and a square metre.

Reading from timetables requires tracking skills. Pupils who do not have this skill will need structured, small step instruction to learn the skill. An L-shaped piece of card may help with the actual process of tracking. Most rail companies have summary timetables giving only two or three destinations. These offer easier tracking tasks.

A number square or times-table square could be used to practise tracking.

Shape and space

The language content around shapes is quite complex. There are some benefits in words like scalene and isosceles in the sense that they are not used in other contexts and with other meanings. There is a considerable new vocabulary to learn and some help may be needed, for example explaining that 'iso' means 'same' and that 'octo' refers to 'eight' as in, for example, octopus.

Some children will find two dimensional representations of three dimensional shapes difficult. Explicit instruction, based on real shapes, should help.

For coordinates, the most likely error will be in mixing up *x* and *y* coordinates. The simple mnemonic 'along the corridor (*x*) and up the stairs (*y*)' may help give the correct order.

Shape and space is a visual topic and must be accompanied by visual teaching materials. Development of this skill is via hands-on materials, for example, pupils should have nets that they can handle and shape before they advance to doing this purely by visualising.

4 Thinking style and mathematics

Introduction

The designers of maths curricula across the world seem to be moving to some similar conclusions, one of which is that the curriculum must encourage flexible thinking. Presumably this is to encourage good problem solving skills in order to complement good computational skills.

However, there is evidence to suggest that there is still an over-reliance on teaching formulas and procedures.

For example, the 2006 Ofsted report *Evaluation: maths provision for 14–19-year olds* noted that: 'Even staff with good subject knowledge often had a restricted range of teaching strategies', and 'Maths became an apparently endless series of algorithms for them, rather than a coherent and interconnected body of knowledge'.[1]

It seems that this has long been the case. In 1971, Skemp observed that:

> The increasing efforts the student makes will inevitably use the only approach which he knows, memorising. This produces a short-term effect, but no long-term retention. So further progress comes to a standstill, with anxiety and loss of self-esteem.[2]

There is a problem, perhaps an understandable one. Procedures, algorithms, are very attractive to both teachers and students, especially when there is an examination dominated ethos in an education system.

Usiskin, in 1998, listed the benefits and attraction of algorithms:

> *Power:* An algorithm applies to a class of problems.

> *Reliability and accuracy:* Done correctly, an algorithm always provides the correct answer.

> *Speed:* An algorithm proceeds directly to the answer.[3]

Many students collude with teachers in accepting the use of algorithms. For example, the mantra for dividing by a fraction, 'Turn upside down and multiply' saves a lot of agony in trying to understand the logic behind the procedure. For examples like this, I can understand why algorithms seduce, but that doesn't mean that I agree!

Formulas, procedures and accurate and swift recall of facts will lead to a version of success in number work, but countries need problem solvers as well as computationally adept pupils (particularly when calculators and computers are readily available).

Two thinking styles

Several researchers have suggested that there are two styles of thinking for maths, extremes at the ends of a continuum. Ideally learners should be able to move appropriately between styles as they solve problems. Two American colleagues and I studied thinking styles, which they had labelled 'inchworm' and 'grasshopper'. Grasshoppers are holistic, intuitive and resist documenting methods. Inchworms are formulaic, procedural, sequential and need to document. The two styles are described and compared in Table 4.1.

Marolda and Davidson (2000), researchers from the USA, also tabulated (Table 4.2) the characteristics of what they call Maths Learning Style I (similar to the inchworm) and Maths Learning Style II (similar to the grasshopper).[4] By describing learning style as opposed to thinking style they take in a broader picture, but describe similar patterns to those in Table 4.1

Table 4.1 Thinking styles of the inchworm and the grasshopper

	Inchworm	*Grasshopper*
First approach to a problem	1 Focuses on the parts and details.	1 Overviews, holistic, puts together.
	2 Looks at the numbers and facts to select a suitable formula or procedure.	2 Looks at the numbers and facts to estimate an answer, or narrow down the range of answers. Controlled exploration (not guessing).
Solving the problem	3 Formula, procedure orientated.	3 Answer orientated.
	4 Constrained focus. Uses one method.	4 Flexible focus. Uses a range of methods.
	5 Works in serially ordered steps, usually forward.	5 Often works back from a trial answer
	6 Uses numbers exactly as given.	6 Adjusts, breaks down/builds up numbers to make an easier calculation.
	7 More comfortable with paper and pen. Documents method.	7 Rarely documents method. Performs calculations mentally (and intuitively).
Checking and evaluating answers	8 Unlikely to check or evaluate answer. If a check is done it will be by the same procedure/method.	8 Likely to appraise and evaluate answer against original estimate. Checks by an alternative method/ procedure.
	9 Often does not understand procedures or values of numbers. Works mechanically.	9 Good understanding of number, methods and relationships.

Table 4.2 Maths Learning Styles I and II

Maths Learning Style I	*Maths Learning Style II*
Highly reliant on verbal skills.	Prefers perceptual stimuli and often reinterprets abstract situations visually or pictorially.
Tends to focus on individual details or single aspects of a situation.	Likes to deal with big ideas; doesn't want to be bothered with the details.
Sees the 'trees', but overlooks the 'forest'.	
Prefers HOW to WHY.	Prefers WHY to HOW.
Relies on a preferred sequence of steps to pursue a goal.	Prefers non-sequential approaches involving patterns and interrelationships.
Reliant on teacher for THE approach.	
Lack of versatility.	
Challenged by perceptual demands.	Challenged by demands for details or the requirement for precise solutions.
Prefers quizzes or unit tests to more comprehensive final exams.	Prefers performance-based or portfolio-type assessments to typical tests.
	More comfortable recognising correct solutions than generating them.
	Prefers comprehensive exams.

The impact of this construct is often under-estimated. It seems obvious that the way that learners think will be a very critical factor in the way they learn and in the way they are taught.

The concept of meta-cognition, sometimes explained as 'thinking about thinking' has been recognised as a major contributor to success in teaching and learning. The National Research Council of the USA published their findings and research in *How People Learn*.[5] They summarise their research in just three key findings, the third of which is: 'The teaching of metacognitive skills should be integrated into the curriculum in a variety of subject areas'.

Hattie's[6] major study of research into what is effective in education found that meta-cognitive strategies were very effective in improving learning. He also mentions within this context the use of self-questioning and states that 'the more varied the instructional strategies throughout a lesson, the more students are influenced'.

The three examples below illustrate thinking styles in operation.

Thinking style and computation

Thinking style will influence how a learner uses numbers and the operations (+, −, × and ÷).

Inchworms see numbers and the symbols for operations literally. In the example below, 98 is seen as just 98, not as a number very close to 100. Indeed if you ask an

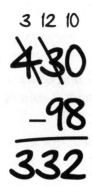

Figure 4.1 Subtraction the inchworm way

inchworm to adjust 98 to an easier number they may not relate to the question and if they do try to answer they may well say 76 or indeed any arbitrary number. They will go into subtraction mode applying the subtraction rules automatically, probably with little or no understanding of the maths behind the procedure (see Figure 4.1).

If the question had been asked as mental arithmetic, then the load on short-term and working memories and visualising the process in the mind would be significant. If the learner has those skills then the method is acceptable, even if not efficient.

The grasshoppers will use their good sense of number values and the interrelationship of operations.

- The 98 will be rounded up to 100 (by adding 2).
- The (simple) subtraction 430 − 100 gives 330.
- The grasshopper knows that this intermediate answer is smaller than the correct answer (by 2).
- Adding 2 takes the grasshopper to the correct answer of 332.

The load on short-term and working memories is less. There is less need to visualise the process in your mind. The method uses good awareness of number values.

Thinking style and problem solving

Which stall at a fair raises £90, if the total raised is £500 and

- tombola takes 34 per cent
- books takes 11 per cent
- cakes takes 23 per cent
- spinner takes 18 per cent
- crafts takes 14 per cent of the total?

An inchworm methodically calculates, starting at the top of the list:

$\frac{34}{100} \times £500 = £170$

$\frac{11}{100} \times £500 = £55$

$\frac{23}{100} \times £500 = £115$

$\frac{18}{100} \times £500 = £90$

A 'spinner' looks at the same question and writes £90. The teacher asks 'Where is your working out?' *'Didn't do any'*, 'So how did you do it?' *'Just knew'*, 'No working, no marks'.

How the spinner did the question was to overview all the percentages and see that among the percentages, only one was a multiple of 9. 18 is a multiple of 9, so 18 per cent must be the answer.

Is that explanation acceptable, even if documented? Teachers' judgements can be influential. They are in a position to sanction methods.

Thinking style and shape and space problems

What is the area of the shaded part of Figure 4.2? (A written answer with method is expected, or a verbal explanation.)

An inchworm with few mathematical skills may well simply count the squares. More mathematically sophisticated inchworms will analyse the *parts* of the figure, seeing a triangle, a square and two thin rectangles. Then, if they bring a knowledge of area to the problem, they may well calculate the area of the triangle from the formula $\frac{1}{2} \times$ base $\times$ height and thus onto the square and the 'legs':

head/triangle	area $= \frac{1}{2} \times 4 \times 4 = 8$	subtotal 8
body/square	area $= 4 \times 4 = 16$	subtotal 24
leg 1	area $= 4$	subtotal 28
leg 2	area $= 4$	**total 32**

The addition of the area of each part is likely to be sequential and irrespective of any number bonds for 10, as in adding a leg to the body to make 20. Inchworms tend not to overview or, indeed look ahead.

On the positive side, the inchworm will be able to document his method, quote formulae and show that, even if he makes an error with the calculation, he has knowledge of area calculations.

The grasshopper may seek to redesign and simplify the problem. He will take an holistic view, trying to put the parts together, so the triangle is 'seen' as half of a 4 × 4 square. The gap between the two legs is also half of a 4 × 4 square, so the triangle can be used to fill that gap and make a 4 × 8 rectangle giving an area of 32. This method is far more difficult for the pupil to document.

A test of thinking style in maths is included in the companion volume to this book, *More Trouble with Maths*.[7]

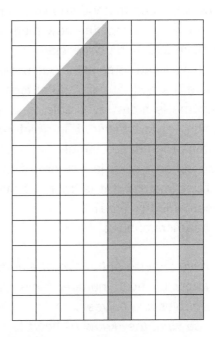

Figure 4.2 What is the area of the shaded figure?

Thinking styles and learning maths

There will be expectations linked with thinking style implications for pupils learning maths. An example is when learners are expected to be able to estimate answers to simple numerical calculations. A more general expectation is that pupils show flexibility in the way they handle maths.

A flexible curriculum will include content which demands both the inchworm style of thinking and the grasshopper style of thinking. Krutetskii (see also Chapter 1), a psychologist and mathematician, specified flexibility of thinking as one of the key requisites for being a good mathematician. The US National Council of Teachers of Maths also lists flexibility as one of the characteristics of good mathematicians. This requirement seems to me to have face validity, that is, it just feels sensible and right. It is possible to survive maths as an inchworm, though there are a number of essential prerequisite skills that are needed to make this an effective style, for example a good long-term memory for sequential information. It is less likely that a grasshopper will survive school maths, especially at higher levels where documentation is essential, but it is likely he will be successful at 'life maths'. So ultimately it may not be the end of the world in everyday life if your maths thinking style is at either extreme, but in the school environment it will, inevitably, be more of a problem. For an adult who can usually avoid some maths, if not all maths, it is less critical to be a flexible thinker, but in general terms as a problem solver, it is going to be better if you can develop flexible thinking. All school subjects teach more than just content. They bring different perspectives and teach different ways of approaching and solving problems. So schools can help and, as ever, awareness of the implications of everything you teach and how you teach it is an important factor. It is back to 'What else are you teaching?'

Many modern maths curricula encourage pupils to share their different methods and for teachers to present different methods for solving problems. This will require good sales techniques from teachers; some pupils will just not want to buy into different methods because they think one method is enough and two or more will be confusing. However, each method should illustrate another facet of the problem and, even if the pupil doesn't adopt the new method, an exposure to a different way of perceiving a problem should be beneficial.

I have listed some of the outcomes that a maths curriculum typically expects of pupils. Where the text is plain, the outcome is inchworm biased, when the text is italic, the outcome is more favourable to a grasshopper thinking style. Underlined text is not thinking-style specific. It is of interest that many of these outcomes form part of the maths programmes targeted at adult learners who have failed to master maths during their school years. Is it 'more of the same' or an inevitable, unavoidable content for learning maths? If it is 'more of the same' can it be presented in a way that makes it learnable this time?

Learners should:

- *have a sense of the size of a number and where it fits in the number system*;
- know by heart number facts such as number bonds (*10*), multiplication tables, *doubles and halves*;
- *use what they know by heart to figure out answers mentally*;
- calculate accurately and efficiently, both *mentally* and with paper and pen, *drawing on a range of calculation strategies*;

- explain the methods and reasoning used using correct mathematical terms;
- *judge whether answers are reasonable and have strategies for checking them where necessary*;
- recognise when it is appropriate to use a calculator and be able to do so effectively;
- *make sense of number problems, including non-routine problems*, and recognise the operations needed to solve them.

Some methods advocated by 'flexible' maths programmes could be classified as grasshopper:

- Exploring all the pairs of numbers that add to make 10. (These are key facts.)
- Approaching mental addition by using the number bonds for 10, for example, $16 + 7$ can be processed as $16 + 4 + 3$ and $22 - 7$ as $22 - 2 - 5 = 15$.
- The four-times-table facts can be obtained by doubling the two-times-table facts. This is an example of *ay* calculated as *bcy*.
- Learning how to add/subtract numbers such as 9, 19, 29 . . . or 11, 21, 31 . . . by adding or subtracting 10, 20, 30 . . . then adjusting.
- Seeing 'easier' numbers within other numbers, for example, $1.5 + 1.6$ is calculated as double 1.5 plus 0.1.
- Finding percentages by halving and quartering and halving again, as in finding 12.5 per cent of £36 by halving three times and in finding 75 per cent of £300 by halving to get 50 per cent, halving again to get 25 per cent and adding to obtain 75 per cent. This is interrelating numbers, building up and breaking down numbers. These values (50 per cent, 25 per cent, 12.5 per cent, 10 per cent and 5 per cent) are key values and can help with estimations.

Some examples of maths topics and objectives that could be classified as inchworm include:

- Knowing facts by heart. The use of long-term mathematical memory, which is a varied ability across the population, to process algorithms (without any understanding).
- Find a small difference between a pair of numbers using counting (but only acceptable for small numbers).
- Using number lines for addition and subtraction.
- Using standard written methods for short multiplication. 'Standard' usually infers methods that are well established, methods that have been around for a long time. Such methods may be familiar to parents, even if some refreshing of the method may be needed. When new methods are introduced, for example, the grid method for multiplication or 'chunking' there is a possibility that parents become disenfranchised and can no longer help their children.

Modern curricula often advocate a mixture of thinking styles (without necessarily articulating this as a policy). Such implications exist in the curiculum statements, for example in Ireland, the maths curriculum of 1999 was structured to 'enable the teacher to cater for individual differences in ability, previous learning and learning style . . .'[8] and in Hong Kong, the curriculum includes:

Fostering general abilities and skills. It is important that students . . . develop their capabilities to learn how to learn, to think logically and creatively, to develop and use knowledge, to analyse and solve problems, to access information and process it effectively and to communicate with others so that they can meet the challenges that confront them now and in the future. Acquiring maths knowledge has always been emphasised, but fostering these general abilities and skills are strongly advocated for all students in the revised curriculum.[9]

Can you change or influence thinking style?

First, you have to ask 'Would it be a good idea?' Basically the wisdom for maths is that learners need to be able to draw on both thinking styles, maybe even in the course of solving a single question, perhaps starting with the overviewing skills of the grasshopper, moving onto the documenting and procedural skills of the inchworm and finally checking the answer using the appraising skills of the grasshopper. Then, some questions and topics lend themselves more to one thinking style than the other, for example, mental arithmetic tends to be better for grasshoppers, while algebra is more inchworm-friendly. So the question becomes can you teach learners to make appropriate use of both styles?

Returning for a moment to the first form of the question, a European study carried out with colleagues in the UK, Holland and Ireland showed that the design of the maths curriculum can have an influence on thinking style. It also showed that many learners can be taught flexible thinking, but, inevitably there will be those who are exceptions. There will be those whose thinking style is so fixed that they can only be taught in that dominant style. For example George was an extreme inchworm. As an eleven year old he would draw, with a ruler and a compass, large, complex and extremely detailed pictures of fantasy army vehicles. Despite more than four years of encouraging flexibility in his approach to maths we had to accept that he was a terminal inchworm. We taught him methods that acknowledged this and he achieved a Grade D in GCSE maths. Typical of his problem solving was a trial and adjust question:

The formula $v = \frac{d^3}{2}$ gives the approximate volume of a sphere.

v is the volume in cm³.

d is the diameter in cm.

A sphere has a volume of 120cm³.

Use trial and improvement to find the diameter, correct to 1 decimal place.

Use the table to record your trials.
The first is done for you.

d	v	
	too small	too big
5		
6		129.6
5.5	91.5	
5.6	98.3	
5.7	105.5	
5.8	113.1	
5.9	121.7	

Figure 4.3 Trial and adjust the inchworm way

As you can see, George had a procedure, which did not include evaluating each trial. He went straight to 6, saw the value it gave for V was too big, but did not evaluate or appreciate how close this value of V was to the target answer of 120. He used his secure inchworm strategy . . . start in the middle, 5.5, and work up, which he did meticulously 0.1 at a time until he arrived (just as the space in the table was about to run out) at the correct answer, 5.9cm.

So, the answer is, 'Usually, yes, but not with everyone'. If you can you should. If you can't then you may do more harm than good and you should teach to the entrenched style. This decision may be linked to the where the learner is in his educational career. If he is approaching a critical examination, such as GCSE then it is too late to try such a change. Impending examinations create different priorities.

During our European study on thinking style we asked pupils as they worked through a set of questions that were designed to diagnose their thinking style, 'How did you do that?' and then a follow up question, 'Can you think of another way to do the question?' After six months in our (specialist) school we retested and the percentage of pupils who could think of an alternative method had more than doubled. Now, our hypothesis was not that the style of teaching was the main cause, though it does lead to increased flexibility over a longer period of time, but that it was mainly the ethos of the classroom which allowed pupils to explore different approaches.

Finally, remember that the uncertain learner often likes the security of the familiar, even if the familiar is not all that successful. Consistency is a key factor in motivation. Teachers may have to do the hard sell on that alternative method.

How do you teach flexible thinking style?

The design of the curriculum is a great influence. If it actively encourages flexibility then most learners will adapt. If it dictates limited methods then most pupils will not explore alternatives. It is a classic example of the interaction between the cognitive and the affective domains.

The ethos of the classroom is another key factor. If learners are encouraged to explore different methods and their efforts are praised and appreciated (children are adept at spotting false praise) then they will generate a learning culture of flexible thinking. Like the CAME[10] programme (Cognitive Acceleration in Mathematics Education), I believe that thinking style teaching should be integrated into the curriculum rather than be taught as a separate skill.

So, pupils can be encouraged to share and discuss different methods. There is a need to manage the extreme inchworms who may be confused by too much choice, but valuing different approaches will encourage flexibility. Once again the culture of speed may be counter productive. If we are encouraging pupils to read, digest, analyse and comprehend questions then the pressure of speed may discourage them from doing that. It should be that there are set times and topics where a more reflective approach is encouraged.

Three key grasshopper skills an inchworm should adopt:

1 Interrelating numbers, for example, seeing 9 as 1 less than 10, seeing 5 as half of 10.
2 Overviewing any problem, for example, reading to the end before starting or getting a feel of what the answer may be.
3 Appraising their answer.

Three key inchworm skills a grasshopper should adopt:

1 Explaining their methods.
2 Documenting their methods.
3 Accepting algebra!

As a first example of teaching pupils to be flexible thinkers while acknowledging potential gaps in subskills, let's take a column addition. Take ten two-digit numbers at random.

      23   Start by eliminating combinations of unit digits that add to 10
      5̶4̶
      74   4 + 6 = 10
      9̶9̶   1 + 9 = 10
      3̶8̶   8 + 2 = 10
      1̶2̶
      6̶6̶
      4̶2̶
      49
    +8̶5̶   5 + 3 + 2 = 10
    ─────
       9   just a 9 left, and a total of four tens (40)

The same strategy is used for the tens digits.
    This method:

● revises the number bonds for 10;
● reduces the risks of addition errors;
● reduces the load on short-term memory;
● and consequently is low stress.

This method is grasshopper in style.
    An alternative method, which is more towards the inchworm style, is to use a mark to represent a ten every time additions go above nine. So, as the units digits are added from top down,

    3 + 1 = 4
    4 + 4 = 8
    8 + 9 = 17

a strike is put through the 9 to represent the 10 and the addition continues with the 7

    7 + 8 = 15

so another strike is used, this time through the 8. The 5 is carried onwards

    5 + 2 = 7   7 + 6 = 13

so another strike is used, this time through the 6. The 3 is carried onwards

3 + 2 = 5
5 + 9 = 14

so a fourth strike is used, this time through the 9. The 4 is carried onwards

4 + 5 = 9, which is written in the units total.

There are four strikes, so 40 is carried as 4 tens into the tens column.
    The same procedure is then used for the tens column.

```
   23
   51
   74
   99
   38
   12
   66
   42
   49
 +85
 ____
  539
```

This method:

- supports short-term memory;
- avoids taking the pupil to any total beyond 19;
- is structured and sequential.

It is also more inchworm-friendly.
    The first method encourages pupils to scan down the numbers and spot the '10s'. The second method is more structured and is less likely to encourage any overview or appraisal of the answer.
    A good question to ask pupils and to support overviewing is to ask them to estimate a total. (There are 10 numbers. If they span the range of 10 to 99 reasonably equally, then an acceptable average is 50 and an estimate is 50 × 10 = 500.)
    As a second example of teaching pupils to be flexible thinkers let's take a word problem about legs . . .

1 On a farm there is a total of thirty-five pigs and chickens. If the total number of legs for these pigs and chickens is 120, how many chickens are there on the farm?

A grasshopper will focus on the numbers involved, that is, 35 and 120. The numbers suggest that the answer is likely to be a factor of 5 and there are likely to be more pigs. So try a 20/15 split (using a trial and adjust approach, but selecting numbers in a logically controlled way rather than just a random choice).

$$20 \times 4 = 80 \qquad 15 \times 2 = 30$$
$$60 + 30 = 110$$

Since this is too few legs and 5 is the factor to consider, move to a 25/10 split to obtain more legs:

$$25 \times 4 = 100 \qquad 10 \times 2 = 20 \qquad \text{Total} = 120$$

There may be no documentation or perhaps just a couple of scribbled numbers. The grasshopper needs to be encouraged to articulate his method and to make notes that communicate his thinking processes.

The inchworm with good algebra skills will set up simultaneous (that is, two) equations:

p = number of pigs $\qquad c$ = number of chickens
$p + c = 35 \qquad$ (based on the number of creatures)
$4p + 2c = 120 \qquad$ (based on the number of legs)

These will then be solved by substitution, say of $p = 35 - c$ into the second equation and the answers will be:

$p = 25$
$c = 10$

The inchworm *may* substitute these answers back into the original question to check their accuracy.

The inchworm needs to be encouraged to make an initial appraisal and an estimate of an answer, even if it is just back at the 'Is the answer bigger or smaller?' which in this case is 'Are there more chickens or pigs?'

The grasshopper overview for question 1 depended on 5 as a factor in the numbers involved. The other encouraging numbers are 1, 2 and 10. There may be a slightly different approach for question 2.

2 There is a total of 42 pigs and chickens on a farm. If they have a total of 126 legs, how many are pigs?

The inchworm will again set up simultaneous equations. If he does not have this skill or the confidence to use this skill then he may try trial and adjust, but the choice of a starting number will be problematic and fairly random. It is unlikely to relate to an appraisal of the numbers in the question.

The grasshopper may well appreciate that the average number of legs for a pig and a chicken is 3 and that $3 \times 2 = 6$, so the number of pigs and chickens is the same (to give the average value of 3) and thus there are 21 of each creature.

If the grasshopper does not sense the answer so precisely, she will still feel that the numbers are near and try the easy split of 22 and 20 and then adjust to 21/21.

If the question now uses 'unfriendly' numbers, then . . .

3 The number of pigs and the number of chickens on a farm add up to 39. The numbers of legs add up to 124. How many pigs are there?

The inchworm will use an algebra solution again. This is ideal for an inchworm, because he has been able to solve all three problems with the same method, providing he has the requisite skills.

There are several trial and adjust style methods for a grasshopper to try. A grasshopper with a less sophisticated skill of controlled exploration may just start with 40 (easier to compute than 39):

$$40 \times 4 = 160$$

He can then adjust back to 39 pigs to obtain 156.

Now appraisal skills can be used to compare 156 with the target number of 124. A difference of 32 legs suggests there should be 16 chickens (if 1 chicken is exchanged for 1 pig, there will be 2 less legs). Thus there are 23 pigs.

A grasshopper may split 39 into 19 and the easy number 20 (but still see the 19 as $20 - 1$).

Then a first trial gives:

$$20 \times 4 = 80$$
$$19 \times 2 = 38$$
$$\text{Total} = 118$$

'Is the answer smaller or bigger?' takes the grasshopper to the decision to add in more pigs. To reach the target number of 124, 6 more legs are needed so there must be 3 more pigs. Thus there are 23 pigs.

In each example the inchworm was able to use the same algebraic procedure. The grasshopper has used a version of trial and adjust, but has usually worked from an initial controlled estimate (which is not a wild guess for this thinking style).

Do teachers have different thinking styles?

I have lectured to teachers about thinking style for many years and usually this involves asking the group to do some maths questions which can be used to diagnose their thinking style. When I ask the group to decide which style predominates for each of them, the show of hands is almost always close to a 50–50 split. It's not sophisticated statistically, but by now it is an extremely large sample!

Another informal survey that was built into my lectures for about three years suggested that different teachers appraise the different styles of thinking of their pupils differently.

A Manchester Metropolitan University study showed that teachers who are not maths specialists but find themselves teaching maths may well regress, out of insecurity, to the formulaic methods they learnt at school, in the same way that insecure pupils do (but see also the Buswell and Judd research).

Teachers need to appraise their own thinking style realistically when teaching maths and appraising maths and look at the pupils who sail through their lessons. Then they should look at the pupils who struggle and see if a mismatch of thinking style is a contributing factor.

The English exam system encourages documentation, which puts grasshoppers at a disadvantage. The multiple choice system used in the USA may interact differently with thinking styles. Lack of documentation in the UK's A-level maths examinations may well result in failure, even if all the answers are correct.

Encouraging flexible thinking style

Flexible thinking should permeate each lesson. Teaching this flexibility should begin at an early age. Some researchers state that thinking style is habitual, but my experience suggests that for many pupils (not all, as ever), thinking style is definitely open to influence. Curriculum can be a significant influence as we found in our tri-country study. Maths curricula need to address a mixture of styles, for example, by interrelating numbers and the four operations. Grasshopper methods make a good overview and introduction. Written methods and a more formulaic approach can be gradually introduced as the curriculum progresses.

One of the other key lessons from thinking styles is to encourage learners to overview and review.

The old teaching adage of 'Tell 'em what you are going to teach, teach 'em, tell 'em what you've just taught them' could infer 'supply an introductory overview, provide a detailed explanation and then review and appraise the whole process and results'. You cover the thinking styles and teach flexibility and thoroughness in working processes.

Different methods should be encouraged, valued and evaluated.

As an example of using different methods consider how the relationship of the numbers can affect the methods used when adding and subtracting. An inchworm will focus on the symbol (+ or −) and move to use a procedure irrespective of the numbers involved. For example faced with 600 − 594 an inchworm is likely to start by using the procedure he has been taught rather than appreciate that the closeness of the two numbers takes him to an easy solution, especially if the computation is done by addition.

Flexible methods for mental addition and subtraction

In each case I have listed the essential subskills needed to succeed when using each method. This may help teachers diagnose where and why a pupil may not be successful in using each method. Again I am trying to help teachers focus on the pupil and what he or she brings to the maths problem.

1 Rounding up, e.g. 98 → 100 or 995 → 1000

For examples where one number is near ten, a hundred, a thousand, etc., such as 758 + 196:

196 is rounded up to 200 and added to 758 to give 998
4 is subtracted to readjust to the addition of 196
giving an answer of 994.

What are the essential subskills?

- An appreciation that you can adjust numbers to make them easier to use.
- A knowledge of the consequences for the intermediate answer of the adjustment, knowing if this intermediate answer is bigger or smaller than the final answer.
- Knowing how to make this adjustment.
- Knowing basic addition facts is less essential in this strategy, but can be used as a check. (In this example, knowing $8 + 6 = 14$ checks the units digit.)
- Remembering the question.

2 Balance and adjust

For example $86 - 38$:

86 is adjusted to 88 by adding 2
$88 - 38 = 50$
adjust back by subtracting 2 to give 48.

What are the essential subskills?

- An appreciation that you can adjust numbers to make them easier to use.
- A knowledge of the consequences for the intermediate answer of the adjustment, knowing if this intermediate answer is bigger or smaller than the final answer.
- Knowing how to make this adjustment.
- Knowing basic subtraction facts is less essential in this strategy, but can be used as a check. (In this example, knowing $\square 6 - \square 8 = \square 8$ checks the units digit.)
- Remembering the question.

3 Counting on

This is an early skill, used for examples such as $9 - 5$, but now involves appreciating how to bridge tens, hundreds, etc.

This method lends itself to modelling with coins (and was used in shops prior to computerised tills).

For example $86 - 38$:

Start with 38 and add to reach 40 (2)
Add tens to reach 80 (40)
Add to reach 86 (6)
Add up the answers from the three steps $2 + 40 + 6 = 48$.

What are the essential subskills?

- An appreciation that you can adjust numbers to make them easier to use.
- Knowing how to make this adjustment.
- Appreciating the significance of the place values of tens, hundreds, etc.
- Knowing how much to add each time, though this can be achieved by counting, but with the potential to affect short-term memory load.
- Remembering the intermediate numbers added on and making the cumulative total.
- *Remembering the question.*

4 Working from left to right

For many pupils mental methods are merely written methods they do in their heads, so adding from left to right will not be a natural inclination.

For example, 374 + 567:

Add 300 to 500 to give 800
Add 70 to 60 to give 130
Add 130 to 800 to give 930
Add 4 to 7 to give 11
Add 11 to 930 to give 941.

What are the essential subskills?

- Knowing addition facts (but counting on is a possibility).
- Remembering the last addition each time.
- *Remembering the question.*

This method has two memory benefits:

- The answer is generated in the correct order of digits.
- The intermediate steps rehearse the intermediate answers.

5 Equal additions for subtraction (also known as 'borrow and pay back')

A method from my own school days.

For example 82 − 57 (although not essential, the sum is usually pictured in the vertical form):

$$
\begin{array}{r}
8^{1}2 \\
-{}^{6}5\text{-}7 \\
\hline
\end{array}
$$

Ten is added to the 2 to make 12 so the units subtraction becomes 12 − 7 (= 5).

An equalising ten is added to the subtracting number so the 50 becomes 60 and the final answer is 25. (I confess that I never knew how this worked, but it did and I got the necessary ticks for my subtractions. I was particularly bemused by the fact that the tens digit of the subtracting number got bigger. I understand now that $x - y$ equals $(x + 10) - (y + 10)$ and will use the method if under pressure to rush out an answer and feel secure about it being correct. Old habits die hard.)

What are the essential subskills?

- A good visual memory.
- Adding in the tens in the correct places.
- Good recall of basic facts (counting on or back is going to push the sort-term memory further towards overload).
- Blind faith in the method!
- An ability to reverse the digits of the derived answer (done from units to hundreds) back into the correct hundreds, tens, units sequence.
- An ability to write the method in an organised and clear form.

6 Using the written algorithm mentally

The learner has to visualise the question as if were written on paper and be able to hold that image and work on it as the computation progresses.

What are the essential subskills?

- A good visual memory.
- Good recall of basic facts (counting on or back is going to push the short-term memory further towards overload).
- Recall of procedures for carrying or decomposing.
- An ability to reverse the digits of the derived answer (done from units to hundreds) back into the correct hundreds, tens, units sequence.
- Estimation skills for a crude check of the final answer. (Failure using this method is likely to be a long way from the correct answer.)

Conclusion

There is almost always more than one way to solve a maths problem, however simple the problem seems to be. Children will become better problem solvers if they can think of 'another way' to solve a problem. This will also help them check their answers and become more confident with their answers. Adults can still learn this skill, though in the case of adults, the skill is probably already there, it just needs drawing out. Learning to leave the old skill behind for a time while you learn another, almost contradictory skill is hard for any sports player. It's hard to do in academic activities, too. The old safe and secure methods are just that, safe and secure. They may be inefficient, but in the early stages of learning the new skill may appear even less efficient. Hopefully that will change and the new skill can take its place alongside the old skill.

The grasshopper style involves the key skill of over-viewing and estimating and the inchworm style involves the key skill of seeing the details and documenting procedures. Encouraging flexibility in thinking style is yet another aspect of the risk taking classroom ethos needed to develop successful, non-anxious mathematicians.

Remember, there may be some inchworms and some grasshopper whose thinking style is terminal and totally impervious to change, however skilled the teacher!

5   Developmental perspectives

Much of maths is developmental. Some psychologists write about a hierarchy of cognitive development, but some aspects of development are simpler than that and others are more sophisticated. Maths is also, largely, a sequential subject. For example, being able to subtract is a prerequisite skill for the traditional 'long' division algorithm.

Whenever a teacher or tutor is working on a maths topic the question 'What else are you teaching?' is very relevant. It may be that a concept is being introduced or that a previously recognised pattern or skill is being revisited in a new form. Each topic is likely to be setting the groundwork for future topics, so there is a need to know where the maths is going as well as where it has come from when taking the first steps on that mathematical journey.

This chapter overviews the links between topics as maths develops. It is hard to teach any topic effectively without knowing where it leads. If the developmental nature of maths is acknowledged in the way lessons are constructed then the progression through the curriculum is likely to be based on understanding and the support for memory that comes from interlinking facts and procedures.

Then there is the issue that Richard Ashcroft and I wrote about some years ago (1993). Maths is made up of parts. 'The parts build on each other to make a whole. Knowing the whole enables one to reflect with more understanding on the parts, which in turn strengthens the whole.'[1]

One of the themes in this book is about the impact of the first learning experience of any new topic and the likelihood that that experience will be enduring whether it is right or wrong.

Consequently at a later stage the question may well change to be 'Where did this problem begin?' If a learner's grasp of the mathematics he has covered so far is not robust or is flawed his learning may break down when faced by a more challenging development.

What does a student need to know before starting a new topic?

One 'simple' aspect of development concerns basic skills and knowledge. For example, not knowing that $6 \times 7 = 42$ would handicap a pupil working on the problem 26×17. The lack of knowledge of a fact is interfering with the learning of a skill. If the marking of this sum is based purely on right/wrong, then a wrong answer is a wrong answer and does not judge that the method has been mastered and that a lack of knowledge of one fact was the source of the error. The feedback is negative. This pupil cannot develop skills in long multiplication without support for his fact retrieval deficit, which, in this example, is the recall of a basic multiplication fact. We as teachers need to be fully aware of the prerequisite skills and knowledge for each new topic, appraise them for the learner and make decisions on how to address them. In this case the intervention may be to supply a table square so that the learner can focus on the process being taught and not have to become anxious about retrieving basic facts.

Considering more learning factors: thinking style (see Chapter 4)

A slightly more complex situation illustrates the multifaceted aspects of progression. Not all learners 'see' problems in the same way. Faced with a question such as 435 − 197 an inchworm and a grasshopper will use quite different procedures to obtain their answers. Each will be drawing on different supporting skills and using different perceptions of numbers. Let's assume that both the inchworm pupil and the grasshopper pupil are skilled in the application of their own particular thinking style.

The inchworm pupil will need a good visual working memory to 'see' the task in his mind as:

$$
\begin{array}{r}
635 \\
-197 \\
\hline
\end{array}
$$

He will then subtract starting at units moving through to hundreds, decomposing/renaming merrily and then reversing the order of the digits from his workings to give an answer of 438. Conceptually he has understood (or at least remembered) the procedure and he has the prerequisite skills, for example, an effective working memory, to carry out the process. He may or may not understand the processes used to deal with decomposing the tens. The experience of success will be down to a combination of prerequisite skills, memory and knowledge. A difficulty in any one aspect of these is likely to result in failure.

The grasshopper pupil will consider the values of the individual numbers and their relative values. He will perceive the 197 as very close to 200 and have a first estimate of the answer as over 400, possibly making a second estimate as a little more than 435. He adjusts for the estimated/approximate subtraction of 200 by adding back 3 to obtain 438. His conceptual understanding has focused less on procedure and more on the relative values of numbers. So, the grasshopper has appreciated the order and size of number by rounding 197 up to 200. He has also understood that the subtraction of 200 gave a smaller answer (compared to subtracting 197) and adjusted by adding 3. His conceptual understanding has focused on the values of numbers.

There is a danger, as ever, of making assumptions. It may be that a grasshopper cannot deal automatically with adding back the 3, but that they can deal with this procedure when it only demands counting on just 1 or 2. This could well be related to working memory capacity.

I think it would be a difficult argument to decide which method was higher up the cognitive development ladder. And that's with taking as an example a relatively straightforward whole number subtraction problem. Neither approach for solving the problem 635 − 197 is wrong. Both have benefits and both need to be taught and understood.

Analysing the ways a task can be approached is a fascinating activity. Any of the cognitive or knowledge factors which are involved in a mathematics task can be a source of the problem; it may be just one factor that is the cause or it could be the interaction of several factors and it may well be influenced by anxiety, attitude and other factors from the affective domain.

Counting and place value

It is dangerous to underestimate the role of place value in maths. It is very influential on the development of maths concepts and skills. When children first learn to count it is usually as an exercise in remembering a sequence of one-digit numbers. Continuing the sequence to the two-digit numbers may disguise the implications of the use of symbols and the order in which they are arranged to represent the words and the quantities they represent. Many children's books about these numbers provide illustrations that are attractive to look at, but give no indication of pattern and inter-relationships, nor of the importance of ten. An ability to recite these numbers is a perfect example of the child giving the parent or the teacher an illusion of learning, of knowing.

There are some additional problems with the inconsistencies of the English language vocabulary (see Chapter 6) for the two-digit numbers. If we put these to one side for now and focus, in this chapter, on the developmental implications.

We use the base ten system, a system based on units, tens, hundreds, thousands and upwards and on tenths, hundredths, thousandths and downwards. There is a symmetry centred on the unit (NOT on the decimal point).

thousands	hundreds	tens	**Units**	tenths	hundredths	thousandths
10×100	10×10	10×1	**1**	$1 \div 10$	$\frac{1}{10} \div 10$	$\frac{1}{100} \div 10$

It is, of course, no coincidence that we have ten fingers, fingers that we often use as tallies for assisting our counting. When we use up all ten fingers, we have to use some form of notation to record that fact before we count on again.

For many years now, I have used the illustration of the sheep counters. It illustrates four aspects of place value, the role of zero as a 'place value holder', crossing the tens, the base ten system and the relationship between addition and subtraction.

The (virtual) picture is of two and then three people, the sheep counters, standing shoulder to shoulder and counting sheep, using their fingers.

The first sheep counter counts the sheep, using one-to-one correspondence, one sheep, one finger, until all ten fingers have been used. He then nudges the second sheep counter (crossing the tens) who displays one finger, but that finger represents ten sheep.

This continues, counting and nudging, until the second sheep counter has used up all ten fingers. He nudges the third sheep counter (crossing the hundreds) who displays one finger. That finger represents 100 sheep, but only if sheep counters one and two are there to create the place value, a value that is dependent on the place the sheep counter holds in the line.

Thus, if there were 16 and then 100 sheep, the sheep counters would show:

16 sheep

100 sheep

Figure 5.1 The sheep counters

If the second sheep counter were not there, the fingers would show 10 sheep. The second sheep counter, showing zero sheep, ensures that we recognise that the third sheep counter is dealing with hundreds. The second sheep counter is the 'place value holder'. He holds the place values in the correct order. There may be 'zero tens' of sheep, but we cannot demonstrate this unless the second sheep counter is there. He (in cooperation with the first sheep counter) makes it clear that the third sheep counter registers the hundreds.

By this deceptively sophisticated model, we can explain how thirty fingers can be used to show nine hundred and ninety-nine sheep. It also demonstrates crossing the tens. That is what the 'nudge' is about.

Should disaster strike the sheep and the numbers start to fall, then there will be a need to 'nudge' in the opposite direction. This demonstrates that addition is in one direction and that subtraction is in the opposite direction. It relates the two operations.

This is an example of developmental teaching. It sets up the concepts that can then be demonstrated by other visual images and materials, for example base ten blocks (used on a place value card) or coins/money (also used on a place value card). As with all materials and manipulatives, it is important to show the symbols, the digits, alongside the material so that the learner can make the links.

The sheep counters demonstration provides a fundamental explanation of place value and the development of addition and subtraction concepts. It remains a viable visual as the maths progresses.

Key facts: the number bonds for 10

10 + 0 = 10	0 + 10 = 10
9 + 1 = 10	1 + 9 = 10
8 + 2 = 10	2 + 8 = 10
7 + 3 = 10	3 + 7 = 10
6 + 4 = 10	4 + 6 = 10

$$5 + 5 = 10$$

These illustrate another aspect of the developmental nature of maths. The second of three key findings of the US National Research Council (*How People Learn*) states that, 'To develop competence in an area of inquiry, students must: (a) have a deep foundation of factual knowledge, (b) understand facts and ideas in the context of a conceptual framework, and (c) organize knowledge in ways that facilitate retrieval and application'.[2]

So, one question, which is especially pertinent for those with poor mathematical memories, is what constitutes 'a deep foundation of factual knowledge'? Well, in maths some facts are more equal than others, or more widely useful. There are some key facts and the number bonds for 10 are truly key facts. They can be presented in a range of images, from rods to fingers to coins, but if they can be learned they will pay back the effort used many times. They can certainly contribute to parts (b) and (c) of the Key Finding Number 2.

At exam times, when anxious pupils may forget even their most carefully remembered facts, it takes only a moment to recreate the figure on p. 83. Note that the anchor fact 5 + 5 is emphasised and used as a check.

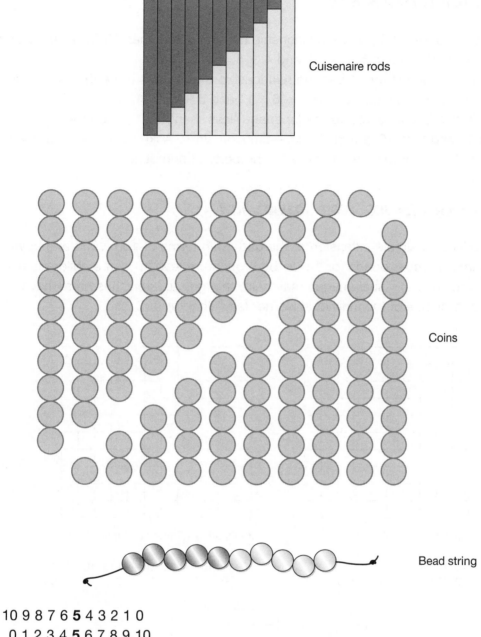

Cuisenaire rods

Coins

Bead string

10 9 8 7 6 **5** 4 3 2 1 0
0 1 2 3 4 **5** 6 7 8 9 10

Figure 5.2 Images of the number bonds for 10

Simple card games, such as pelmanism can be used to practise these facts. The facts should be remembered as addition facts, for example 6 + 4 = 10, but also as missing addends, for example, 6 + □ = 10, a presentation that is a foundation for algebra and also leads to the subtraction fact, 10 − 6 = 4.

Extensions and development of the number bonds for 10

These eleven facts can be developed into many more facts. By anchoring any new facts back to the number bonds for 10, the learner has a check and, once again, number facts are being inter-related. Some examples of extensions from these facts are:

Number bonds for 9 and 11

The number bonds for 9 use the relationship that 9 is 1 less than 10. Thus, for example 5 + 5 = 10 is adjusted to 5 + 4 = 9 and 4 + 5 = 9.

The number bonds for 11 use the relationship that 11 is 1 more than 10. Thus, for example 5 + 5 = 10 is adjusted to 5 + 6 = 11 and 6 + 5 = 11.

Even in this simple exercise the language 'less than' and 'more than' is revisited. Relating 11 and 9 to 10 is reinforcing estimation skills. Acknowledging that 9 is both 5 + 4 and 4 + 5 revises the commutative property of numbers.

Number bonds for 100, 1000, 10,000 and 1

This introduces a simple extension of the pattern in terms of 100, 1000 and upwards. The (decimal) number bonds for 1 may be a quantum leap for some children. In each extension the use of visual images may help, though, as ever, these may have to be the personal choice of the individual learner (see Chapter 9).

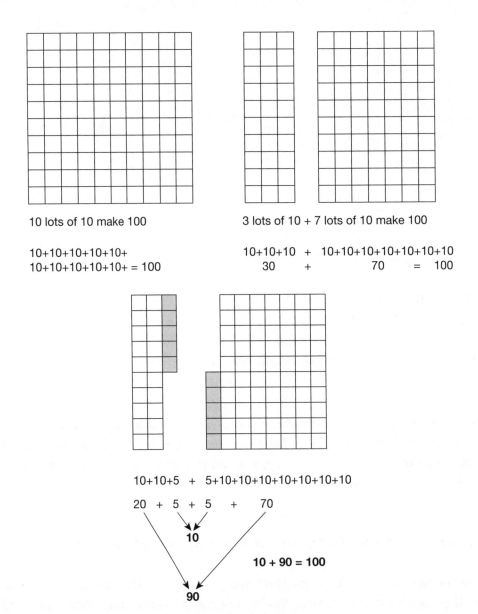

10 lots of 10 make 100   3 lots of 10 + 7 lots of 10 make 100

10+10+10+10+10+   10+10+10 + 10+10+10+10+10+10+10
10+10+10+10+10+ = 100   30   +   70   =   100

10+10+5 + 5+10+10+10+10+10+10+10

20 + 5 + 5   +   70

10

10 + 90 = 100

90

Figure 5.3 Number bonds for 100 with base ten blocks

The extension from 7 + 3 to 70 + 30 is fairly straightforward, though we should not underestimate the challenge that multiplying and dividing by powers of 10 creates for some learners (a place value issue again). The extension to 75 + 25 requires a revisit to 10 as 9 + 1.

The extension to 0.3 + 0.7 could be modelled with 10p coins, after establishing that 10p is 0.1 of £1, 20p is 0.2 of £1 and so on (calculators 'remove' the end 0 from 0.10 and 0.20 to make them 0.1 and 0.2).

Estimation

The understanding of 10 and its neighbouring numbers helps set the foundations for estimation skills. So, knowing that '9 is close to, and smaller than 10, 8 is close but less close than 9, 11 is close to and greater than 10, 12 is close but less close than 11' can be extended to numbers around 90, 900, 0.9, 0.09, and so on. Visual images could be base ten materials or money, with money more representative as the coins and notes are not proportional to the values they represent. Money, of course, takes us into everyday maths.

Adding by casting out 10s

A column of numbers can be added by casting out combinations that make 10. For example

```
59
34
92   2 + 3 + 5 = 10
33
81   1 + 9 = 10
75
+48  casting out the 2, 3, 5, 1 and 9 leaves only 8 + 4,
───  which could, if strategies were forgotten, be quickly counted on.
422  Then 3 (10s) are 'carried' over to the tens column.
```

The procedure can be repeated for the tens column, casting out 8 + 7 + 5 = 20, 3 + 3 + 4 = 10, leaving 9 + 3 = 12. Adding up these tens gives 42 tens, which is 420.

This method encourages the learner to overview the numbers rather than just start to add from the top number.

When working out an average (mean) learners have to add a group of numbers. This method may enable them to do that accurately, so that any problems with the addition subskill of working out an average is circumvented.

Subtraction

Number bonds for 10 and 100 are especially useful once again when subtracting, particularly if this is done by counting on through tens, hundreds and thousands.

It is also useful to remember the number bonds in 'subtraction' format, for example as with

$4 + \square = 10$

Remember: Revision of basic facts can be done in many topic settings, for example with angles. Number sums for 90° and 180° allow learners to practice addition and subtraction skills in a new context.

A developmental sequence based on addition and multiplication

If we understand some of the development of mathematical ideas we are better able to diagnose where difficulties lie because we can track back until we find the root of the problem. For example, for the development of multiplication skills and concepts and their relationship to addition, a sequence could be:

$7 + 7 + 7$
7×3
$17 \times 3 = 3 \times 10 + 3 \times 7$
$37 \times 23 = 20 \times 37 + 3 \times 37$
$v + v + v = 3v$
$2v + v = 3v$
$q + q + q + r + r = 3q + 2r$
$5y + 2y = 7y$
$4y + 2w + 3y + w = 7y + 3w$
$b = w + y$
$ab = a(w + y) = aw + ay$
$(a + w)(b + y) = ab + ay + bw + wy$

This is not a definitive sequence, but illustrates how, for example, algebra is rooted in very early experiences of number. It also illustrates how a dependence on counting in ones will handicap progression. If learners are stuck at the counting in ones stage they will not comprehend that numbers are about quantities, quantities that can be understood in an holistic way rather than as a collection of ones or tallies. So, for example, 3×5 can be viewed as 'three lots of five' and thus $5 + 5 + 5$, which could be computed as 5, 10 then 15, adding on 5 for each step. For the learner who remains at the 'ones' stage then the addition has to be done by adding ones, as in:

5 . . . 6, 7, 8, 9, 10 . . . 11, 12, 13, 14, 15

Because there are so many steps this could result in errors, even though the learner has a sense of security about using ones. It is inefficient, and increasingly so as the numbers become larger. It will also prevent the learner from seeing patterns and understanding concepts, including algebra.

A 12 year old extends her use of counting:
$2/5 + 3/8 = 18$

It can be valuable to consider the developmental sequence backwards as well as forwards. Some may not see 7 × 3 as a true member of a developmental sequence, but merely as a basic fact, but if your strategy to access 7 × 3 is 7 × 2 plus 7 (× 1) then it is very much an early member of the sequence. The common themes in the sequence are multiplication as repeated addition and multiplication by using partial products. The underlying operation in this developmental sequence is addition.

7 × 3 is 7 + 7 + 7, which can be grouped as 7 + 7 (7 × 2) and 7 (7 × 1)

17 × 3 can be seen as 10 × 3 plus 7 × 3, based on 3 + 3 + 3 + 3 + 3 + 3 + 3 + 3 + 3 + 3 + 3 + 3 + 3 + 3 + 3 + 3 + 3

37 × 23 is often computed from two partial products 37 × 3 and 37 × 20 where the 37 × 20 is computed as 37 × 10 × 2

v + *v* + *v* is algebra for, for example, 7 + 7 + 7, leading to 3*v* and its equivalent 7 × 3

q + *q* + *q* + *r* + *r* becomes 3*q* + 2*r*

5*y* + 2*y* is the algebra version of 5 × 3 + 2 × 3 and become 7*y*

4*y* + 2*w* + 3*y* + *w* illustrates the grouping of like terms as 7*y* + 3*w*

a(*w* + *y*) requires that both *w* and *y* are multiplied by a to give *aw* + *ay* which is another algebra version of 7 × 3 as 7(2 + 1) and also a reminder of the commutative property – that is, 7 × 3 = 3 × 7

(*a* + *w*)(*b* + *y*) is the algebra version of 37 × 23 as (30 + 7)(20 + 3) and the understanding of this could well have begun at 7 × 3, linking multiplication and addition and grouping additions to make partial products.

(All the above examples can have an associated simple area diagram to emphasise the common theme, for example Figure 5.4.)

Some learners are not only stuck in the 'counting in ones' developmental stage, they are stuck in the 'counting in ones forward' stage. They are not able to master the 'counting in ones backward' stage, which sets the foundation for subtraction.

Times-tables facts and developmental maths

Some people find rote learning and recalling these 121 facts a virtually impossible task. If they persevere in trying to rote learn them then anxiety increases while self-confidence decreases. The times-table facts are important facts which make a very large contribution to numeracy. If it is possible to rote learn and retain them then they should be learned. Their use pervades maths curricula as is illustrated below for the single fact 3 × 7 = 21:

3 × 7 = 21
3 × 17
38 × 47
30 × 70
300 × 700

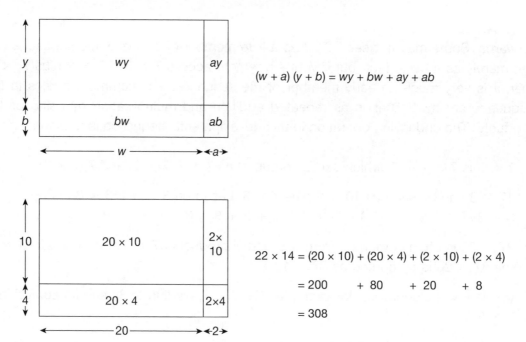

$$(w + a)(y + b) = wy + bw + ay + ab$$

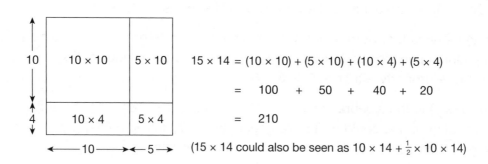

$$22 \times 14 = (20 \times 10) + (20 \times 4) + (2 \times 10) + (2 \times 4)$$
$$= 200 \quad + 80 \quad + 20 \quad + 8$$
$$= 308$$

$$15 \times 14 = (10 \times 10) + (5 \times 10) + (10 \times 4) + (5 \times 4)$$
$$= \quad 100 \quad + \quad 50 \quad + \quad 40 \quad + \quad 20$$
$$= \quad 210$$

(15 × 14 could also be seen as $10 \times 14 + \frac{1}{2} \times 10 \times 14$)

$$7 \times 8 = (5 \times 8) + (2 \times 8) = 40 + 16 = 56$$

Figure 5.4 Area models for multiplication

and for division

$$3\overline{)6210}$$

and for multiplication and division in two steps

$$45 \times 21 = 45 \times 3 \times 7 \qquad 756 \div 21 = 756 \div 3 = 252 \div 7 = 36$$

and for fractions

$$\frac{2}{3} + \frac{1}{7} = \frac{14}{21} + \frac{3}{21} = \frac{17}{21}$$

and decimals

$$0.3 \times 0.7 = 0.21 \quad 0.03 \times 0.07 = 0.0021$$

and percentages

$$30\% \text{ of } 70 = \frac{30}{100} \times 70 = 21$$

and money

$$3 \times 7p = 21p$$

$$3 \times £7 = £21$$

and measures

$$3 \times 7g = 3 \times \frac{7}{1000}\,kg = 0.021\,kg$$

and negative numbers

$$-3 \times -7 = +21$$

and shape and space

$$\text{Area} = l \times b = 3m \times 7m = 21m^2$$

and algebra

$$a + a + a = 3a \qquad b + b + b + b + b + b + b = 7b$$
$$3a \times 7b = 21ab$$
$$x^2 + 10x + 21 = (x + 7)(x + 3)$$
$$x^2 + 4x - 21 = (x + 7)(x - 3)$$

and word problems

Mike buys three pens at 7p each. How much does he pay?
How many days in three weeks?

The ability to access this collection of facts is an essential prerequisite for developing maths concepts and skills.

The multiplication facts can be taught (but, as is ever thus, not for all pupils) by rote learning, but that reduces them to just being facts, when the concept of multiplication can be taught by introducing strategies that can be used to access the answers for these 'basic' facts. The difficulties with rote learning these facts can be turned into a positive and beneficial learning experience for students by introducing them to the use of strategies which also illustrate several maths concepts.

How to teach times-table facts to students by using developmental maths

The following suggestions use developmental methods which are based on the grasshopper skill of breaking down and building up numbers. Inchworm learners need to know how to use that skill. In fact, the strategies are sufficiently consistent for most inchworms to adapt to them. This can only increase awareness of flexible ways to learn maths. The strategies also have the benefit of setting conceptual foundations for future topics including long multiplication and division and algebra. These may not be appreciated by the grasshopper who is often intuitive, so there is a benefit for both thinking styles in experiencing a structured approach to this topic. These approaches help develop a better sense of number which is so useful for everyday-life maths, too.

The principles

- Use the easy facts (1×, 2×, 5×, 10×) to work out the harder facts, that is, build on what is known. These are key facts to add to those other key facts, the number bonds for 10.
- Use two easy steps when one step is too hard. This will become inevitable later in maths as the numbers being multiplied become bigger.

Many learners do not realise that there are only twenty-one facts that have the reputation for being harder to learn.

First put the problem into perspective. Learning (by rote), or more accurately forgetting these facts is an issue. Newspapers love it, 'Back to basics . . . *everyone* will learn their tables' (and presumably move onwards and upwards thereafter). Adults with selective memories say 'We all learned them. We sat and chanted them till we did'. All this mythical nonsense piles on the pressure for those who don't achieve success in this particular task, A teacher may well have the double task of teaching the multiplication facts and restoring the learner's self-esteem so that he believes that he can succeed in maths. So let's put the numbers into perspective . . .

A table square for the 0× to 10× facts has 121 facts for multiplication (and 100 for division). A blank square (Figure 5.5) looks daunting to fill, but if the facts for 0, 1, 2, 5 and 10 are filled in then there are only 36 facts left (Figure 5.6). Six of these are the squares (32, 42, 62, 72, 82, 92). The remaining 30 may be halved to fifteen due to the commutative property of $ab = ba$. So there are twenty-one remaining facts after we master the 'easy' ones.

	0	1	2	3	4	5	6	7	8	9	10
0											
1											
2											
3											
4											
5											
6											
7											
8											
9											
10											

Figure 5.5 The blank table square

	0	1	2	3	4	5	6	7	8	9	10
0	0	0	0	0	0	0	0	0	0	0	0
1	0	1	2	3	4	5	6	7	8	9	10
2	0	2	4	6	8	10	12	14	16	18	20
3	0	3	6			15					30
4	0	4	8			20					40
5	0	5	10	15	20	25	30	35	40	45	50
6	0	6	12			30					60
7	0	7	14			35					70
8	0	8	16			40					80
9	0	9	18			45					90
10	0	10	20	30	40	50	60	70	80	90	100

Figure 5.6 The almost complete table square, with the 'easy' number facts entered

(For full details of the methods described below and mature, non-childish graphics try my book *What to Do When You Can't Learn the Times Tables*.)

The vocabulary chosen will have a great influence on understanding.

For example, 3 × 6 is also 6 + 6 + 6. This is 'three lots of six (added)' where the words say (almost) what you write. Also this version can be demonstrated with materials. The phrase 'three times six' is abstract and the learner has to be able to interpret the maths language.

These three sixes can be grouped as (6 + 6) + 6 or (2 × 6) + 6, where the repeated addition has been shortened to the addition of 'easy' chunks or partial products.

Similarly, 7 × 8 is also 'seven lots of eight' 8 + 8 + 8 + 8 + 8 + 8 + 8, which can be grouped as (8 + 8 + 8 + 8 + 8) + (8 + 8) or 'five lots of eight' plus 'two lots of eight' or (5 × 8) + (2 × 8).

This can be extended to a two-digit multiplier such as 12 × 4, which is also 'twelve lots of 4' 4 + 4 + 4 + 4 + 4 + 4 + 4 + 4 + 4 + 4 + 4 + 4 or 'ten lots of four' plus 'two lots of four' (10 × 4) + (2 × 4).

Deriving 'hard' facts by using the easy facts . . . a summary:

- 9× derived from 10× using a straightforward pattern (which also teaches estimation and subsequent adjustment).
- 4× derived by doubling the 2× facts (teaching cumulative multiplication, such as 30× as 3× followed by 10×).
- 3× derived by partial products 2× plus 1× (which can be used as an introduction to using partial products and thus the basics of 'long' multiplication).
- 6× derived by partial products 5× plus 1×.
- 7× derived by partial products 5× plus 2×.
- 8× actually only 8 × 8 is left, so just keep doubling till you reach 64! (which reminds students that 8 is 2^3).

More detail

9×

The pattern is, for those who can deal with some algebra, that $9n = 10n - n$. This can be demonstrated with Cuisenaire rods (9 and 10) arranged as area, as in Figure 5.7.

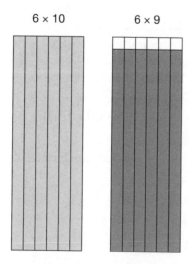

6 × 10   6 × 9

Figure 5.7 6 × 10 compared to 6 × 9

Each 9 is 1 less than each 10, so for example, six lots of nine are six less then six lots of ten (which makes quite a memorable pattern).

$$6 \times 9 = 6 \times 10 - 6 \qquad\qquad 60 - 6 = 54$$

And to check that this is correct, add the digits in the answer, $5 + 4 = 9$. It's a checking rule that works for any number times 9, for example:

24 lots of 9 are 24 lots of 10 minus 24
$24 \times 9 = 240 - 24 = 216$ (and to check, add the digits in 216 ... $2 + 1 + 6 = 9$)

So, there is another pattern. The digits of the answer will always add to 9 (useful as a check and for division to find out if nine is a factor).

This procedure also teaches estimation ($\times 10$) and how to refine the estimation. For the refinement, the question, 'Is the answer bigger or smaller?' is once again apposite.

$4\times$

Double twice, for example:

4×7 start with $2 \times 7 = 14$
then double again, $2 \times 14 = 28$

As with the 10 strategy for 9 ($9n = 10n - n$), the double-double strategy for 4 works with numbers beyond the table square collection.

The developmental uses of this double-double strategy are illustrated below, starting with the algebraic generalisation, illustrating again the 'What else are you teaching?' facet of this approach.

If $y = ab$ then $wy = w \times a \times b = wab$

For example,

6×4 use $\times 4$ as $\times 2 \times 2$	$6 \times 2 = 12$	$12 \times 2 = 24$
34×6 use $\times 6$ as $\times 3 \times 2$	$34 \times 3 = 102$	$102 \times 2 = 204$
31×20 use $\times 20$ as $\times 2 \times 10$	$31 \times 2 = 62$	$62 \times 10 = 620$
67×300 use $\times 300$ as $\times 3 \times 100$	$67 \times 3 = 201$	$201 \times 100 = 20{,}100$
71×0.2 use $\times 0.2$ as $\times 2 \div 10$	$71 \times 2 = 142$	$142 \div 10 = 14.2$
$248 \div 4$ use $\div 4$ as $\div 2 \div 2$	$248 \div 2 = 124$	$124 \div 2 = 62$ (and $\div 8$ just takes one more step. See below.)

$248 \times \frac{1}{8}$ use $\times \frac{1}{8}$ as $\div 2 \div 2 \div 2$　$248 \div 2 = 124$　$124 \div 2 = 62$　$62 \div 2 = 31$
$84 \times \frac{2}{3}$ use $\times \frac{2}{3}$ as $\div 3 \times 2$　　　　$84 \div 3 = 28$　　$28 \times 2 = 56$

The use of two steps may be an indispensible strategy for mathematical mortals.

3×, 6× and 7×

Use partial products:

so $3 \times 8 = 2 \times 8$ plus $1 \times 8 = 16 + 8 = 24$
and $3 \times 6 = 2 \times 6$ plus $1 \times 6 = 12 + 6 = 18$
and $6 \times 6 = 5 \times 6$ plus $1 \times 6 = 30 + 6 = 36$
and $6 \times 8 = 5 \times 8$ plus $1 \times 8 = 40 + 8 = 48$
and $7 \times 8 = 5 \times 8$ plus $2 \times 8 = 40 + 16 = 56$ (and did you know that 56 = 7×8 has the digits 5678 in order?)
and $7 \times 6 = 5 \times 6$ plus $2 \times 6 = 30 + 12 = 42$

This strategy has introduced the procedure for 'long' multiplications, the use of partial products, for example:

23×51
becomes 20×51 plus $3 \times 51 = 1020 + 153 = 1173$

This, the distributive law, can be generalised via algebra and some of its developmental aspects summarised as

If $y = a + b$ then $wy = w(a + b) = aw + bw$

For example,

$3 \times 5 = 5 \times 3 = 5(2 + 1) = 5 \times 2 + 5 \times 1 = 10 + 5$

$6 \times 8 = 8 \times 6 = 8(5 + 1) = 5 \times 8 + 1 \times 8 = 40 + 8$

$12 \times 13 = 13 \times 12 = 13(10 + 2) = 10 \times 13 + 2 \times 13 = 130 + 26 = 156$

$17 \times 9 = 17(10 - 1) = 17 \times 10 - 17 \times 1 = 170 - 17 = 153$

$42 \times 99 = 42(100 - 1) = 4200 - 42 = 4158$

15% of $440 = (10\% + 5\%)$ of 440 and $44 + 22 = 66$ (5% of 440 is half of 10% of 440)

75% of $440 = (50\% + 25\%)$ of 440 and $220 + 110 = 330$ (25% of 440 is half of 50% of 440)

$52 \times 81 = 81 \times 52 = 81(50 + 2) = 81 \times 50 + 81 \times 2 = 4050 + 162 = 4212$

$40 \times \frac{3}{4} = 40(\frac{1}{2} + \frac{1}{4}) = 20 + 10 = 30$ ($\frac{1}{4}$ of 40 is half of $\frac{1}{2}$ of 40)

$68 \times 0.55 = 68(0.5 + 0.05) = 34 + 3.4 = 37.4$ (0.05×68 is one tenth of 0.5×68)

The area model

Just a reminder that these multiplications can be shown by an area model (see Figure 5.4, p. 88).

Multiplication facts later in the curriculum (or life)

Multiplication facts are just a set of facts that are stored in memory. If they are accessed by strategies such as those described in this chapter then the retrieval of a multiplication fact may also be a skill, which also has to be remembered. If a fact is not used regularly then it will be less prominent in the memory. The same is true if a skill is not practised regularly. However a skill, because it is usually applies to many examples, is likely to be practiced or accessed more often than a specific fact.

This note of caution applies, obviously, to many other areas of mathematics and is a most important reason to use a spiral structure for the mathematics curriculum, and a spiral with a small pitch to ensure frequent returns to the previous levels.

Multiplication facts and examinations

Examinations always put extra pressure on insecure learners. For many such learners extra time may be granted for the examination. One use of extra time is to write down key information at the start of the examination before anxiety kicks in at full intensity. Learners can be shown how to draw up a times-tables facts square quite quickly and efficiently, drawing on the linking strategies described above. It will be a great help if they are allowed to take squared paper into the examination, then all they have to do is fill in the 'easy' facts, 0×, 1×, 2×, 5×, 10×. This provides a 'skeleton' table square (see Figure 5.6). Then, on demand, a 4× fact can be computed from a 2× fact, a 9× fact from 10× fact, a 3× fact by adding 2× and 1× facts, 6× facts by adding 5× and 1× facts and 7× facts by adding 5× and 2× facts. One gap remains, 8 × 8, which can be computed by multiplying by 2 as 2^3.

The easy multiplication facts, long multiplication and long division

Traditional long multiplication is multiplication using partial products. For example, 782 × 43 would be done as 782 × 40 plus 782 × 3. Similarly traditional long division is done by subtraction of partial products, for example 6919 ÷ 37 will start with a subtraction of 3700 (37 × 100) then subtraction of 2960 (37 × 80) and finally 259 (37 × 7), to give an answer of 187. In both these examples the learner has no choice of partial product. The method dictates which ones to select. In the multiplication, the partial products are based on place values. In the division example, they are based on factors, in this example these are 100×, 80× and 7×. This may be a problem if the learner has weak and possibly inaccurate recall of 8× and 7× facts.

Alternative structuring of multiplication and division by partial products using the 'easy' numbers is shown in Chapter 3. These methods relate multiplication (more obviously) to repeated addition and division to repeated subtraction (or repeated addition for those who retain their barriers to using subtraction).

It should be noted that these methods, sometimes referred to as 'chunking' are the same as the 'traditional' methods, which also add together or subtract 'chunks'. In these variations the 'chunks' are based on 'easy' multiples. The methods also relate back to the strategies described for accessing the basic facts of multiplication, described earlier in this chapter. The 'chunks' are, of course, actually partial products. The methods also allow for estimations.

Levels of learning

Returning to the introductory paragraph of this chapter and the psychological inter-pretation of developmental mathematics, a number of psychologists from Piaget to Gagne have looked at levels or hierarchies of learning. This complements the discussions above on the developmental nature of mathematics, which has considered development from a maths content perspective. Gagne (1977) described four levels of learning.[3]

Associative (rote) learning

Associative learning is establishing a memorised response to the presentation of a stimulus. It focuses on memorisation and mastery. For example, pupils learn the six times table and can respond '42' automatically when asked 'What is 7×6?' or a teacher demonstrates short division and pupils then practises ten examples of short division.

Concept learning

Concept learning occurs when children attempt to identify characteristics that determine inclusion in or exclusion from a set or class. It focuses on categorising, classifying, ordering and labelling. For example, children learn that $\frac{1}{2}, \frac{4}{5}, \frac{71}{99}$ and $\frac{5}{3}$ can all be classified as 'fractions' or pupils know that both the drawings below contain *three* items:

Principle learning

Principle learning occurs when children attempt to relate ideas. For example, pupils use the distributive property ($5 \times 7 = 5 \times 5 + 5 \times 2$) in new situations such as

$$5 \times 34 = 5 \times 30 + 5 \times 4$$

Problem solving

Problem solving occurs when children employ principles to achieve a goal. It focuses on applying, verifying and proving. Pupils must both select and apply certain principles in order to arrive at a solution. They integrate skills, concepts and principles into a cognitive structure. For example, in solving a word problem such as,

Mike and Sam decide to share the cost of a Coke and a packet of crisps. Coke costs 45p and crisps cost 35p. How much does each boy pay?

Bruner (1966) identified three types of knowing that are also pertinent:

- Enactive knowing is kinaesthetic and tactile.
- Iconic knowing is visually or mentally image-related.
- Symbolic knowing is abstract.

Conclusion

Mathematics is a very developmental subject. Facts develop, procedures develop and concepts develop. The foundations are set with the early experiences. Concepts start to build with these early experiences and equally misconceptions may start to build in these early times, too. So, from a pre-emptive perspective, it is important to minimise the misconceptions by being aware of where they may occur and where the current work will lead mathematically. From the intervention perspective it is important to be able to look back and be aware of where the foundations for the current work were set, where the gaps are and the implications of those 'holes' for the learner.

So taking a developmental perspective means being able to look forwards and backwards at the learner and each 'new' maths topic. It also reminds us to look for 'What else are you teaching?'

6 The vocabulary and language of maths

I've given a separate chapter to this topic because it causes difficulties for so many children. In fact I know that this is an area of maths that needs a lot more research.

Communication is about language. How teachers explain ideas, how learners understand them is highly dependent on language. One of the factors in communication is, obviously, vocabulary. In maths, another key communication factor is the use of symbols, such as + and ÷, which introduces another layer, the need to relate symbols to vocabulary and to concepts.

In the early stages of learning maths, many difficulties are largely a consequence of the peculiarities and irregularities of many maths words in the English language, for example, the use of the same words and phrases (such as 'take away') in everyday life as well as for maths can be a source of confusion. Later it is a consequence of the way word problems are written and constructed. So the problems and confusions are both with the vocabulary of maths and with the language (semantics) of maths.

Several writers have commented on the bizarre nature of word problems and students' attitudes to them, for example, Jo Boaler[1] has noted, 'Students come to know that they are entering a realm in which common-sense and real world knowledge are not needed', and the consequence of this is, 'Students learn to ignore contexts and work only with the numbers'.

As an example of problems with the vocabulary in the early stages of maths, consider the next nine two-digit numbers after 10. They start with eleven and twelve which are exceptions, one-off words, then they take the digit order and reverse it as in 13 as thirteen, 14 as fourteen, and on to fifteen, sixteen, seventeen, eighteen and nineteen. Thirteen and fifteen compound the eccentricity of the teen numbers by not being 'threeteen' and 'fiveteen', and of course all of these words end in teen rather than ten. The twenties, thirties and beyond then fall into a pattern where the words tally with the digit order, although thirty, forty, fifty, sixty, seventy, eighty and ninety as words are irregular in the sense that they are not three ten, (threety would be a step in the consistent direction) four ten and so on as happens with one hundred, two hundred, three hundred and so on. This inconsistency does not help children develop the patterns that would help them understand this first exposure to place value.

There can be a further problem with the vocabulary here. Consider the '-teen' words and the '-ty' words, for example, thirteen and thirty. The end syllable of both words has a similar sound. Learners with poor auditory discrimination may not hear that subtle difference and learning may become blurred. There is a similar issue of potential confusion with words such as 'hundreds' and 'hundredths'. It's hard to understand when you don't recognise the vocabulary.

As an example of a language comprehension difficulty we have word problems such as, 'Mark has two more toys than James. Mark has ten toys. How many toys does James have?' The key vocabulary that normally hints at the operation '+' is 'more', one of several words we can use to infer addition, but here the question requires a subtraction, 10 − 2. So, having taught the child that the vocabulary for + can be said as 'add, more, plus or and' he then meets 'more' used in the language of a maths question where the interpretation has to be 'subtract'.

So, the main difficulties and confusions in the words of maths come from two aspects, vocabulary and semantics and then in the interpretation and comprehension of the language used to write mathematics word problems.

The teen numbers (and eleven and twelve)

As mentioned above, the teen numbers are probably the first inconsistency (see also Chapter 8) in the language of maths that children meet. The numbers from 11 to 19 do not have names that fit the pattern of later numbers. For example, compare thirteen with twenty-three, thirty-three, forty-three and so on to ninety-three. 13 is said as 'unit-ten', 23, 33 and so on are said as 'ten-unit', that is, in the same sequence as the digits. While we often take pains to encourage children to look for the pattern, we should warn them of this particular exception. Basically they have to learn the first nineteen numbers as exceptions to the rule before they can start to look for a pattern. Most children simply absorb the information by repetition. Unfortunately, the teen numbers occur frequently in everyday life. The fact that children can deal with this irregularity by constant exposure to the information may well hide their underlying confusion.

So, this vocabulary issue may lead to uncertainty or even confusion in the child's first experience of two-digit numbers, and thus the key concept of place value. Even when the learner realises the situation and mostly manages to stay correct, when using these numbers within a longer calculation, the lack of automaticity may well create errors by reverting back to the first, incorrectly learned information. For example, one of the other, not surprising, consequences of the order of the components of teen words is that pupils may transpose numbers. For example they may write 51 for fifteen. It may help to use manipulatives such as base ten blocks or coins to reinforce the correct order of digits or arrow cards (Figure 6.1) or claim that the teen numbers are as difficult as teenagers.

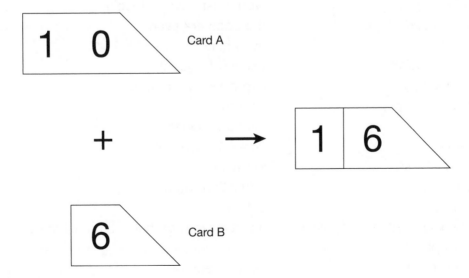

Figure 6.1 Place value arrow cards

The 'dual' vocabulary of maths

The vocabulary of mathematics is full of examples of inconsistencies, and as has been said before, insecure learners do not like or cope well with inconsistencies. The colloquial nature of some maths vocabulary, that is words used in mathematics that are used with different meanings in everyday non-mathematical language, is a good example of pupils having to adjust to inconsistencies, in this case in the meaning of a familiar word.

Children have to learn that some words and phrases they have been using in everyday language have a specific meaning when used in a maths context, for example, they may meet 'sort, match and count' in very early maths and then, later, 'operation and capacity'. There are some more examples below:

acute (angle)	acute (pain)
angle	what's your angle?
anti	auntie
borrow (in subtraction)	borrow (lend)
bracket ( )	bracket for a shelf
by, as in 6m by 8m	by the river
	'Bye, bye'
cancel (in fractions)	cancel a ticket
capacity (volume)	capacity (potential)
carry (addition)	carry a bag
chord (circle)	chord (music)
clockwise	streetwise
compass (NESW)	compass (circle)
count (1, 2, 3 . . .)	Count Dracula
count on (in numbers)	count on me
degree (°)	degree (BSc)
difference between two	difference in appearance
numbers (subtraction)	
digit (number)	digit (finger)
divide (÷)	the path divides
double (×2)	'you must have a double'
even numbers	the odds are even
	even him!
expand (brackets)	expand (balloon)
expression $(xy + 3)$	expression on a face
face (on a shape)	your face
	face on a clock
factor $(15 = 5 \times 3)$	factor 15 sun screen
formula $(d = st)$	Formula 1
function $f(x)$	a function room
goes into	enters
half $(\frac{1}{2})$ with 'half' as a precise	half a pizza with 'half' as an estimate
concept	
heavy (weight)	heavy metal
hour	our

index (x^3)	index (book)
	index finger
interval (data)	interval (theatre)
key (calculator)	key (symbol)
	key (idea)
	key (lock)
	quay
left (right)	'left' as in subtraction ('how many are left?')
light (weight)	light (bulb)
makes (equals)	makes (a cake)
mass (in kg)	mass (in church)
match (compare)	strike a match
mean (average)	mean (nasty)
	I didn't mean that
mixed number	aren't most numbers mixed?
multiple of 5	multiple injuries
negative (−7)	negative (critical)
net (flat pack)	net (fishing)
	net (not gross)
odd numbers	odd person
	odd you should say that
operation (+, −, ×, ÷)	operation (hospital)
	operation (military)
order	last orders
	religious order
	order (command)
place value	value of a place (in the sun)
plane	plane (747)
	plane (wood)
	plain
pi	pie
pound (£)	pound (lb)
	(dog) pound
	pound (pummel)
power	(world) power
	power (strength)
prime (number)	prime (location)
prism	prison
product (6 × 7 = 42)	product (manufactured)
proper/improper	yes
range	Range (Rover)
	range (shooting)
reduced to . . .	reduced to tears
reflex (angle)	reflex (doctor and rubber hammer)
relationship between numbers	relationship between people
remainder	remainders (bargains)
	reindeers

remove (the brackets)	remove (literally)
	remove (take away, but not subtract)
right angle	wrong angle
roughly (close)	roughly (playing)
round (up or down)	round the garden
	round the block
	round (circular)
rule (obey)	metre rule
scale (1:10)	scale (weighing)
second place	60 seconds
share (÷)	Cher (!)
	share (stock exchange)
show your working	show you're working
sign (as in ÷)	sign (road)
simplify (algebra and fractions)	simplify (make easier)
solution (solve)	solution (dissolve)
solve (the equation)	solve (the murder mystery)
sort (arrange)	sort (you out!)
substitute (in algebra)	substitute (soccer)
sum	some
symmetry	cemetery

'two lines of symmetry' or 'two lines in a cemetery'

table (data)	table (and chairs)
take away (subtract)	take away (food)
tall (height)	tall story
term (ax)	term (school)
third (3rd)	third ($\frac{1}{3}$)
times	*Sunday Times*
	old times
	good times
total	total darkness
translation	translation (language)
triangular number (value)	triangular numer (shape 4)
units (tens, hundreds)	industrial units
week	weak
weight	wait

This is not a small problem.

So, do not assume that the learner will automatically adjust to the new, maths meaning of a word and enter into the maths world where it lives. They may be distracted by their original understanding of the word. They may be misled and diverted from the idea you are trying to purvey.

The four operations

Inconsistencies arise with the basic operations, $+$, $-$, $\times$ and $\div$. Even the word 'operation' is more usually associated with hospitals rather than with maths lessons. Perhaps because adding, subtracting, multiplying and, to a lesser extent, dividing are 'everyday' maths operations, they have attracted a varied vocabulary. So we can infer $+$ by 'plus, add, more, increase, sum, total, and, in all, all together'. The learner has to cope with a choice of several words for the same maths operation. Some pupils, especially those with special needs, like consistency, so if they have internalised 'plus' as their word for $+$, then they may find difficulty in accepting 'and'.

These 'four operations' words have a second problem associated with them. As outlined previously, many are not exclusive to maths and may also have more than one meaning in maths, for example 'plus' can mean 'positive' or a bonus as in 'That's a plus'. This particular example is also clouded by the use of -8 to mean 'minus or negative 8' while we do not write the $+$ sign for 'positive or plus' 8 when using integers.

Eight-year-old girl: 'It's cold today. It's take away 5 degrees.'

These are well recognised confusions. For example Anne Henderson[2] has examined this language aspect of maths, but the flexibility of vocabulary can be something to celebrate, too, and pupils could be asked 'Can you think of another word we can use for this?'

Decimals

This is another similarity problem for some learners, akin to the '-ty' and '-teen' problem. The learner needs good auditory discrimination to hear the difference between ten and tenth, hundred and hundredth, thousand and thousandth. The sounds are similar, but the numbers they label are very different. This could be the one time that the 'slower and louder' intervention technique actually might be appropriate! But it is a very good time to combine visual and oral presentations of information. Once again, materials/manipulatives can redirect the learning.

Little words, especially 'not'

Some of the learners who have weaker reading skills miss the little words when reading, such as 'and' or 'not'. Missing 'not' is a drastic error! It may help to use a highlighter pen for the little words, so that they are less likely to be overlooked.

Homophones

Another source of potential confusion and ineffective communication are homophones, words that sound the same as another, different word, for example, in this mental arithmetic problem:

Aziz ate four of his eight apples. How many were left?

we have 'ate' and 'eight' and 'four', which could be 'for' as in 'Aziz ate for England!'
Other homophones include:

one	won
two	to, too
by	buy
complementary	complimentary
key	quay
plane	plain
prism	prison
sine	sign
sum	some
weight	wait

Again these issues may attack the fragile security of the learner.

Word problems

Singapore has once again ranked in the top performers (2nd) in maths in the 2009 PISA (Programme for International Student Assessment). The *Singapore Model Method for learning mathematics*[3] has made a significant contribution to this success. (See Chapter 9 for more on the Singapore Model Method.)

Their heuristics for problem solving in primary and lower secondary school maths are:

- act it out
- use a diagram/model
- make a systematic list
- look for pattern(s)
- work backwards
- use before–after concept
- use guess and check
- make suppositions
- restate the problem in another way
- simplify the problem
- solve part of the problem
- think of a related problem
- use equations.

Writing word problems

The potential for variation in word problems is enormous. This makes teaching them more of a challenge. Unlike computations where there is every chance of teaching all the possible variations, this is not the case with word problems. Again, my experience in lecturing and training around the world is that this is an international problem. For example, Bryant, Bryant and Hammill (2000) surveyed 391 teachers of children with maths weaknesses on which topics in maths caused them the most concern. The first three items of thirty-three concerned word problems and the language of maths.

Pupils usually meet word problems where they have to translate words to symbol sentences or equations. *It is very useful for them to practice the opposite translation, that is, symbols to words so that they can learn how a word problem can be composed.*

So, for example, they could be asked to create a word problem for 8 − 3:

> The key words for subtract are (see Henderson)[4] 'less, left, minus, take away, subtract, difference' . . .
>
> A very basic statement would be, 'What is 8 minus 3?'
>
> This can be reworded to, 'What is 3 less than 8?' or 'What is left if I take 3 from 8?'
>
> Or 'Take 3 away from 8' or 'Subtract 3 from 8'.

In all of these, the order of the numbers is now 3 . . . 8. This can create difficulty for insecure learners. They could however, be used as an early example of the skills needed to interpret word problems, especially the need to overview before starting to solve the problem.

> '8 take away 3' or 'What is the difference between 8 and 3?' (Note: 'difference' is often misinterpreted as questioning the difference in appearance.)

These return to a number order of 8 . . . 3.

But then children can be encouraged to add in more vocabulary and language variables. The following examples show how the complexity of vocabulary and language can be increased while the computation remains the same.

- Basic — 8 minus 3
- Wrong order (mathematical) — Subtract 3 from 8
- Objects — Sam has 8 *toys*. Mike takes 3 *toys* from Sam. How many *toys* does Sam have left?
- Big words — *Samantha* has 8 *chocolate digestive biscuits*. She eats 3. How many are left?
- Two key words — Jay has lost some coins and has 8 *left*. He loses 3 *more*. How many coins does he have now?
- Superfluous data — Kev has 8 coins. *Mike has 6 coins*. Kev loses 3 coins. How many has he left?
- Words for numbers — Tia has *eight* cans of cola. She drinks *three*. How many has she left?
- No familiar key word — Jon juggles 8 balls. He drops 3. How many is he juggling now?
- Wrong key word — Zak has eight cakes. He gives three cakes to some friends. How many *more* cakes can he give to his friends?

● Two stage and superfluous

Jon has twenty pairs of socks. Six pairs are blue. Four pairs are white. Two red pairs have holes in them. The other pairs are green. All his socks fit size 11 feet. If Jon gets three green pairs wet, how many pairs of green socks are dry?

Pupils can be guided towards increasing complexity and creativity, thus, hopefully, understanding how word problems are constructed.

In addition to coping with the flexibility of vocabulary for the four signs, $+$, $-$, $\times$ and $\div$, pupils will meet questions where the words are deliberately used to have an opposite meaning taking us again into semantics. Students need a strategy that goes beyond just highlighting the key word and relating it to the usual operation. So, back to writing word problems . . .

For example, the pupils' task could be to write a word problem where a word such as 'more' is used first to infer addition and then secondly to infer subtraction. This is often a matter of just changing the order of the other words.

1   Jon has three toys. Sam has two more toys that Jon. How many toys does Sam have?

   $3 + 2 = 5$

2   Sam has three toys. Sam has two more toys than Jon. How many toys does Jon have?

   $3 - 2 = 1$

And a different order for 'less':

3   Jon has three toys. Sam has two less toys that Jon. How many toys does Sam have?

   $3 - 2 = 1$

4   Sam has three toys. Sam has two less toys than Jon. How many toys does Jon have?

   $3 + 2 = 5$

Interpreting word problems

1   Pictures
   Because language is so variable and word problem writers are so creative (in a stilted sort of a way), one of the best strategies is to illustrate the problem by using simple drawings. This strategy makes the student read the problem carefully and then interpret it in a visual mode.

   Jon: ✈✈✈   Sam: ✈✈✈ + ✈✈

   (a) Jon . . . 3 toys   Sam . . . Jon's toys (3) and 2 more makes 5

   Who has more toys?   *Sam*

   Sam: ✈✈✈   Jon: ✈ (✈✈)

(b) Sam . . . 3 toys   Sam has two more toys than Jon, so Jon has 2 less

Who has more toys?   *Sam*

The illustrations should be backed by the key question, *'Is the answer bigger or smaller?'* now slightly rephrased as, 'Who has more toys (Jon or Sam)?'

2 Reword the question
   As in 'Who has more toys?'

3 Selecting the operation(s)
   As in 'Is this add, subtract, multiply or divide?'

4 Throwing in a guesstimate and evaluating the outcome. Does it make sense?

Then there are the questions that not only require the student to decide on the operation, but also require them to abandon common sense. Many students do not relate maths questions to the same reality as a teacher, so in the example below, the question setter is anticipating 32 ÷ 5 followed by rounding up 6.4 to 7. A 12-year-old pupil wrote her answer as '32'. One could make an argument in support of that answer. So the common sense that was required was as expected by the question setter, not the common sense as applied by the student.

   Sophisticated, but disguised maths content:

   If cars take 5 people, how many cars would be needed to take a group of 32 friends to a concert?

Different shapes, different words: the vocabulary of shape and space

Some of the vocabulary around shape and space topics is quite exclusive, and hence may alienate the learner. For example, there are a number of words to describe different four-sided shapes.

   Do these help pupils to understand what makes a shape different? For example, ask students to arrange these words in a logical sequence and then justify their decision.

   QUADRILATERAL, SQUARE, TRAPEZIUM, RECTANGLE, PARALLELOGRAM, KITE, RHOMBUS

Now do the same for triangles.

   ISOSCELES, EQUILATERAL, SCALENE, RIGHT ANGLED, ACUTE ANGLED, OBTUSE ANGLED

Links

Some words can be linked to meanings that are familiar thus using the everyday/maths links as a help with the maths meaning. I have left space for your own and your pupils' link words and phrases.

cent	century centipede centurian percentage
circumference	fence circling a field (see also perimeter) . . . circum means round and 'ference' could be said very quickly so that it sounds like 'fence'
complementary (angles)	complete the straight line
concave	going into a cave
cosine (also sine and tangent)	There are some well known 'poems' built around these and opposite, adjacent and hypotenuse. It would seem that the more inclined to innuendo, and the less subtle the content, the better the memory!
decagon, decimal	decade decimate ten
equi	equal
mega	megastar (big . . . one million)
milli	millennium millimetre (There is a potential for confusion here. A millennium is one thousand years, a large number of years. A millimeter is one thousandth of a metre, a small distance.)
mode	model, modern . . . most popular
octagon	octopus . . . eight
percentage	per: *divide*; cent: *hundred*
perimeter	a perimeter fence (and the per does not mean divide)
quadrilateral	quad bike . . . four

Add your own and your pupils' link words and phrases

Using units

Speed (and velocity) can be linked via their units *miles per hour or kilometres per hour or metres per second.* As with percentages, 'per' means divide. The units are combining a distance unit and a time unit with division, so a speed unit is a (distance unit ÷ time unit).

The same works for density, although the units are less familiar than those used for speed. The units are gram per cubic centimeter or kilogramme per cubic metre . . . (mass unit ÷ volume unit).

The instruction words

These need to be taught, demonstrated and explained. Pupils need to understand what they imply mathematically. They include:

● calculate
● compare

- convert
- correct (as in 'to 2 decimal places' and not as 'absolutely correct')
- estimate
- evaluate
- expand
- explain
- express
- factorise
- find
- invert
- investigate
- prove
- round
- simplify
- solve.

Conclusion

Communication via language is not as simple as it might seem. For example, some words used in maths come with a previously learned alternative meaning. (This is yet another example of the influence of first learning experiences.) The inconsistencies of vocabulary can confuse mathematically and handicap the development of conceptual understanding. As with many of the different aspects of maths, assumptions are dangerous. With verbal communications and instructions, the assumption that what you say is what the learner hears may only be true at the literal level rather than at the understanding level.

As some books say . . . 'x is the unknown' . . . Spooky!

7   Anxiety and attributions

[G]ave up. I can't sink strate I always get two answers.

(Twelve-and-a-half-year-old male student attempting a question sheet on basic division facts)

In many senses this is a chapter that brings together all the other chapters. If everything else about the learning is considered, for example, acknowledging weak working memory or providing appropriate worksheets, anxiety, attitude and attribution can still generate failure. Failure can be specific to a topic, a lesson or even part of a lesson, but unrecognised and unaddressed failure at any stage in maths has serious consequences for future learning.

Maths seems to be THE subject for creating anxiety. Books have been written about maths anxiety. I have known adults who have been driven close to depression by an unavoidable maths task. Even the memories of maths lessons in school can generate anxiety in some adults – a Danish friend remembers her maths lessons:

I am sitting in my room looking at the open maths book, getting ready to do my homework. All I can see are the numbers on the paper, numbers that frighten me and make me sad.

I keep sharpening my pencils again and again, constantly writing and erasing my answers making the pages in my maths book almost unreadable. Most of the pages are full of my teacher's red and blue notes. Everything I have written has been wrong.

The teacher's comments are filling as much space as are my attempts to please him and live up to his far too high expectations. I know that tomorrow I will again have to face humiliation in the classroom.

He will look at our homework and ask me questions he knows I cannot answer. I will try to make myself invisible again, but he will find me, asking me another impossible question. Everyone will look at me and he will say loudly, 'Let's ask someone who will know the answer.'

It is not what he is saying that hurts me, but it is his harsh voice, his hostile body language and angry expressions, his cold staring eyes, his angry stamping on the floor, his way of saying my name, his tight angry lips, the hard finger poking my back while he yells out loud, blaming me for not being able to do mathematics.

It's a scenario one hopes would be rare today, but maths anxiety doesn't always need so much extra help (!) from a teacher, the subject itself is enough for many learners. Within this story there are several important clues as to the influence of maths anxiety. It illustrates an interesting concept from Martin Seligman, an American psychologist, the concept of 'Attributional Style'.[1] Basically Attributional Style is the way we attribute reasons and causes to the events that happen in our lives.

Let's take a closer look at this scenario.

All I can see are the numbers on the page, numbers that frighten me and make me sad.

The visual impact of a page of numbers can be almost terrifying for some learners. They know that numbers relate to failure and that a lot of numbers relate to a lot of failure. (I feel much the same about many of the forms I had to fill in when I was a Headteacher. Many people feel that way about their tax return.) The numbers also make her sad and that is a deeper emotion, more permanent.

I keep sharpening my pencils again and again.

'Busy work' that delays starting work on the maths. (I did the same with those endless forms, but my avoidance strategy was to make coffee after coffee.)

constantly writing and erasing my answers

The learner is not committing to a final answer. Sometimes they will not commit to any answer at all, that is they just will not write anything.

making the pages in my maths book almost unreadable.

Another way to avoid producing work that can be marked as wrong, but it risks further critical comments from a teacher.

Most of the pages are full of my teacher's red and blue notes.

The teacher is giving feedback that confirms the learner's sense of inadequacy. I helped organise a conference and activity day for teenage dyslexic learners a few years ago. One of their recommendations for teachers was that they should mark neatly, discretely and with a dark pen (that is not red). Negative feedback does not encourage pupils to take the risks necessary to become learners.

Everything I have written has been wrong.

The learner feels that the problem is pervasive. *Everything I have written* . . . This leads to a sense of helplessness, that there is nothing to encourage her.

The teacher's comments are filling as much space as are my attempts to please him and live up to his far too high expectations.

Once again the feedback is reinforcing the learner's sense of inadequacy. The teacher is telling the student that it is all her fault. This comment also introduces 'expectations'. Setting expectations at just the right level, not too low, not too high, and constantly adjusting them is a very demanding skill. Learners are surrounded by expectations, from governments through to peers.

I know that tomorrow I will again have to face humiliation in the classroom.

The learner has a sense of pessimism and permanence.

The remaining two paragraphs graphically describe a person who is being taught by a teacher who should not be teaching. Every interaction described reinforces, powerfully, the helplessness of the learner. There is nothing to lead her out of her attributional style. The maths is no longer the issue.

The learner will start to form beliefs that then lead to an attributional style that has an impact on all future attempts to learn, for example:

- *I'm no good at maths. I never will be.* Permanent and personal.
- *I can't do fractions. I can't do any maths.* Pervasive and personal.
- *I hate fractions. I hate all maths.* Pervasive.
- *I don't read well. I'm hopeless at word problems.* Pervasive and personal.
- *People who like maths are weird.* Personal (an attribution that takes away the need to be good at maths).
- *I don't like maths. I don't know anyone who likes maths.* Personal (another attribution that takes away the need to be good at maths).
- *Only really clever people are good at maths (therefore I am not clever).* Personal.

Listening to what learners say and hearing their words in the context of attributions can tell you so much. There are questionnaires that identify the facets of attributional style, but everyday talk gives diagnostic clues and clues that are on-going. The examples above illustrate this idea.

Anxiety

Anxiety is not always a bad thing. It is said that facilitative anxiety motivates and alters behaviour positively whereas debilitative anxiety inhibits or alters behaviour negatively. The impact depends on the degree of anxiety and the make-up of the individual. However it is usually debilitative anxiety that we meet in maths.

Factors contributing to maths anxiety

Several factors may contribute to anxiety in maths, for example:

- A poor understanding of maths.
- A poor memory for maths facts and procedures.
- The abstract nature of maths.
- Inappropriate instruction (for example, instruction that does not differentiate for the range of learners in a group, or instruction that does not acknowledge memory issues).
- Badly designed work tasks, for example, content beyond the learner's capabilities or over-designed, overcrowded worksheets.
- A curriculum that does not take account of the range of learners at whom it is targeted.
- A curriculum without sufficient differentiation.
- Constant under-achievement or failure.
- Teachers' attitudes.

- Parental attitudes.
- The pressure of having to do maths quickly (and we have to ask, 'What is the rush?' 'Where did this come from?').
- The extreme judgemental nature of maths, that is, answers are almost always judged as 'right' or 'wrong'. Having to attempt something where you think you will fail creates anxiety.

A survey into anxiety among secondary age students (11 to 17 years)

My research into maths anxiety in students in England was published in 2009.[2] It surveyed over 2000 secondary students and 440 dyslexic secondary students. These students were presented with 20 situations such as 'Doing long division problems without a calculator' 'Taking an end-of-term maths exam' and 'Showing your maths report to Mum or Dad' and were asked to grade each one as:

1 'Never a problem'
2 'Sometimes'
3 'Often'
4 'Always'

The results showed that there were no significant differences for males and females, not in average scores and not in the rank order of the items. The dyslexic students were all from special schools and should, therefore, have experienced appropriate teaching. Their average score and ranking of the items was very similar to that for the mainstream students. The two items that were ranked higher for them were remembering the times-table facts and doing long multiplication questions without a calculator.

What was very interesting were the items that came at the top of the ranking and the items that came bottom of the ranking. 'Taking an end of term maths examination' was the top anxiety issue for everyone. 'Doing long division questions without a calculator' came high as did 'Having to do maths questions quickly'. 'Working out my money when shopping' came very low in the ranking.

The culture of having to do maths quickly is very detrimental for children with learning difficulties (and, as this survey showed, disliked by many children who do not have learning difficulties). One characteristic that is commonly found across the learning difficulties spectrum is slow processing, so the speed culture of maths is discriminatory. However, the 'Having to do maths quickly' item in my survey was ranked high for *all* students.

One of the reasons behind doing the survey was that listening to the learner and doing something about what you hear improves educational outcomes (see Hattie)[3].

I made an arbitrary decision that a total score for the twenty items of 60 (averaging 3, which is 'often') or above indicated high anxiety. On this basis the indication was that about 5 per cent of students from this survey have high maths anxiety. Of course all the ratings of the items in the questionnaire are subjective. This survey does not have the precision of number fact answers.

The anxiety questionnaire will feature in the companion book *More Trouble with Maths*.

The 'no answer'

In the 1990s I did a study on the errors that dyslexic secondary school pupils made in maths computations. A good example was 12.3 + 5, where the most common error was to add the .3 and the 5 to give an answer of 12.8. The percentage rate of this error was almost identical for the dyslexic pupils and the non-dyslexic pupils. The same was true for all computational errors in this no time limit test. However, there was one error that stood out as different for the two groups and that was the error of the 'no attempt'. The 'no attempt' means, not surprisingly, that the pupil simply does not attempt the question. The answer space is left blank, no answer, no working. Dyslexic pupils exhibited this reaction far, far more frequently than the non-dyslexic pupils.

The reason was explained to me by a dyslexic student who went on from my school to obtain a degree in maths ... 'If I know I am going to fail to answer the question correctly, I don't try. Then no one can say to me, "Never mind, you did your best". If I do my best I want to succeed, not fail.' This behaviour is about not risking failure.

Failure rarely motivates. Recently I have been asking the teachers who attend my lectures, 'At what age are enough pupils giving up on maths for you to notice?' I have asked this question across the UK and in many countries around the world. The sample must by now run into thousands. The modal answer is 7 years in virtually every country. Does this mean that, by the age of 7 years, some children have experienced enough failure to give up? If so, what can we do as educators to address that problem? It also tells me that maths learning problems are an international phenomenon.

So, back to the 'no attempt'. Look for the no answers, the blank spaces in work. They are almost as diagnostic as the written or spoken errors. An optimistic interpretation may mean the learner is insecure in that topic and it maybe that all that is needed is a little time to review the topic or maybe just reassurance. It may be that the learner needs some scaffolding, such as a multiplication fact square. Of course it could also mean that the learner has a total blank on that topic, but at least you are taking a more refined diagnostic approach than merely appraising attainment via a summarising mark such as $\frac{4}{10}$.

Risk taking

Most learning involves risk. A baby taking its first steps is taking a risk. Some people are natural risk takers across all aspects of their lives. Others have areas where they are natural risk takers but other areas where they are cautious to the 'no-attempt' level. For example I will take the risk of lecturing to a large audience, but I am firmly in the no-attempt camp for any roller coaster that does 360° loops.

Maths probably discourages risk taking more than any other school subject. It is just so very judgemental.

It will be the classroom ethos that encourages or discourages risk taking in maths. The teacher who dramatically gives a large red ink cross for an incorrect question is not encouraging future risk taking. He has just upped the risk stakes for the learner. The teacher who says 'Close, just not quite right, ... but close, ... if you do this, ... change this, ... check that fact, ... just read this bit again and tell me what you think it means' or similar phrases is encouraging risk taking.

The pupil who just sits there and is supremely reluctant to start work may well be an ultimate, but hopefully not terminal, risk avoider.

Risk taking and thinking style

As ever, there are interactions between the different factors introduced in Chapter 2. There is an interaction between thinking style and anxiety.

A classroom study I was involved in, working in three European countries with 11–13-year-old pupils with specific learning difficulties (SpLD) and non-SpLD controls, looked at their thinking styles in maths. The finding that is relevant for this chapter is that the SpLD group made very much more use of the formulaic/instrumental/inchworm style than their non-SpLD peers. We hypothesised that the reason for this was that the students' perception of the inchworm style was that, even though it often made demands they could not handle, such as sequential memory, it seemed safer. This perception is often confirmed by those teachers who endorse and sanction inchworm learning. A further consideration that supports this hypothesis is the fact that the holistic and flexible methods favoured by grasshopper thinkers offer too much choice and thus generate insecurity and inconsistency. So many of the facets of learning discussed in this book interact.

Current trends in maths are encouraging pupils to generate different methods and to understand the maths they are doing. This seems to be an international trend in maths curricula. But, as ever, there are implications in how it is done. Most importantly is an acceptance (active, not passive) by teachers that this can happen and a classroom ethos that encourages flexibility without frightening those pupils for whom flexibility is never going to be an option. I do not know what percentage this may be, but I guess around 5 per cent.

And inclusion encourages us to consider all children, not just the 67 per cent that are in the middle part of the normal distribution.

Expectations

Pupils are surrounded by many different sources of expectations. Some of these expectations may be conflicting, for example those of a peer group versus those of a teacher. Many pupils are adept at constantly adjusting to these surrounding and conflicting expectations. However there will be times when certain expectations take on a dominant role. Examinations are a prime example.

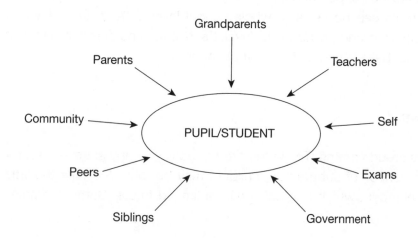

Figure 7.1
Expectations

Pupils are sometimes subject to expectations based on other family members. These may be verbalised by teachers. 'Your sister was just superb at maths' or 'Your brother was useless at maths'. The pupil failing in maths may be all too aware of their successful (and even worse, younger) sibling.

There will be cultural expectations. A few years ago females were not expected to do as well as males in maths (irrational). A group of boys may have a culture of not trying in maths, which may be partly to avoid failure while preserving an image or may be just rebellion or perhaps the peer group does not have an acceptable image of pupils who do excel in maths.

In the current educational culture there is a fashion of setting targets, which are really just formally presented expectations. I have had concerns about this trend to set targets for individual pupils, unless they are short term and constructed in consultation with the student, mainly because this is such a very skilled task and is subject to so many uncontrollable variables that (as a physicist) the accuracy of any target is dubious at best. Perhaps underlying all these expectations is, and few of us are privy to this secret, that the Government's target is that all children should be above average. That would shock PISA.

My starting analysis is that if the target is too easy, some learners will simply cruise, or worse, stop when they feel they have achieved the target. But, if the target is too high and perceived as unachievable then it de-motivates the student. There are so many factors to consider, as always, and learners do not provide a stable or consistent base. If he's tired, had a row with his girlfriend, his football team lost or he's busy memorising the lyrics of a chart song, maths may not be the priority at that time. Wrapping up the whole process in mushy acronyms (for example, SMART) does not act as a substitute for appropriate teaching nor significantly reduce the hazards associated with the process of setting targets.

However, I do feel that expectations are the key to success. It's just that the bureaucrats have hijacked the idea. Expectations are linked, among other things, to attributional style. Teachers need positive, encouraging, nurturing attributions and they need to communicate them to their learners in a way that permeates all of their lessons. Expectations need to be fluid and adjustable. They often need on-going fine tuning if they are to be achieved and exceeded. So, when you write a target or an expectation, let the child and the circumstances dictate the outcome and then manage the consequences of that outcome.

When I taught in the USA, I met a word that fitted my need, an adjective that, although ungrammatical, turned a dubious concept into a acceptable one. The word was 'un-anxious' and thus 'un-anxious expectations'.

Expectations or targets can be set at a whole school level, a year group level, a classroom level, a lesson level and an individual level. Each should be different in format and expected outcomes, but they should be complementary.

Beliefs and maths

There are many beliefs around maths. These tend to be rooted in early experiences, for example, in early experiences of subtraction, children may be told 'You take the little number from the big number', which is a belief with a limited future. Some examples of beliefs are:

- Mathematics problems have only one answer (but then the possibility of more than one answer creates a sense of uncertainty for some learners).
- In maths word problems, the relative size of numbers is more important than the relationships between the quantities they represent. (So, if the numbers are relatively close in value they are added or subtracted. If they are relatively far apart in value then they are multiplied or divided.) This eliminates the need to try and understand the problem!
- Mathematics is a collection of facts, rules, procedures and formulas (which is sometimes the way it is taught and sometimes the way it is perceived).
- You have to be really brainy to do maths (and thus 'not normal').

Some learners see beliefs as inviolate, others see them as a challenge. As ever, the individual does not have to match the 'average'.

Anxiety, self-confidence and attributional style: intervention and prevention

Addressing anxiety, self-confidence and a negative attributional style is not likely to be a quick process. The chances are that the problem has built up over a long time and that it will only be reduced over a long time. There are some basic classroom strategies/ philosophies for promoting pupils' self-confidence in learning maths and thus guide their attributional style to be more optimistic and positive:

- Tell pupils that effort is important (learned-helpless pupils believe there is little relationship between effort and success) and then make sure that you reinforce this in comments, marking and any feedback to the pupil. Encourage self-efficacy.
- Tell pupils that their own improvement is more important than doing better than other pupils.
- Make sure pupils experience genuine success in maths and avoid patronising praise, especially when directed at the learner rather than at the success in a task.
- Give challenging tasks that show that being wrong is a part of the learning process, but control the impact of the mistakes by direct and personal encouragement. Trial and adjust questions are a relatively secure way of doing this. Estimation tasks can also help. Some coursework can teach this lesson. Again some acknowledgement of the level or stage at which the learner feels secure and/or appropriate intervention may be needed.
- Promote pupil's self-confidence in learning maths by giving positive and constructive feedback.
- Praise the work, not the child. That way any hiccups can be dealt with by appropriate attributions, rather than being taken personally.
- Create a classroom ethos that encourages involvement by:
  - creating an ethos of meaningful praise (I prefer lots of 'little praises' to fewer 'big praises');
  - creating a classroom ethos that encourages learners to take a risk.
- Remind pupils that learning involves risk and make sure that the consequences of taking a risk are not negative.

Do we teach algebra so that each new generation can share a common experience in maths, that is 'I can't do algebra!' (and I guess the same could be said of fractions)?

Attributional style

Building a positive attributional style appeals to me. I feel that it is a more robust outcome than just building self-esteem or self-confidence. It seems to set firmer foundations and have a more lasting influence.

A poor attributional style is the result of constant negative feedback, perhaps internal as well as external, something that is more than likely for a weak maths student. The negative feedback comes from many sources, the teacher, in what he says and how he says it, in what he doesn't say, how he marks and appraises work, peers and the learner's status within the peer group, parents' reactions to reports, and the learner's own frustrations and failures, real or imagined.

Seligman's interpretation of how people attribute their successes and failures is so apposite for maths learning. The three aspects of attribution are:

1 Pervasive . . . 'I can't do this sum, I can't do any maths.'
2 Permanent . . . 'I couldn't learn the times-table facts last night. I'll never be able to learn them.'
3 Personal . . . 'It's all my fault, I'm just too stupid to do maths.'

It takes time and that constant drip, drip of negative feedback to make attributions become negative, so it should be no surprise that it takes time and a lot of positive drips to turn those attributions around.

Addressing attribution should be an integral pat of all lessons. What students say often tells you which attributions are in play. Once again, it's about listening to the students.

Professor Bob Burden conducted a study on students at my school on their self-concept and self-efficacy.[4] It was published in 2005 by Whurr (now Wiley). The students came out well!

Conclusion

This could be the most important topic in this book. Maybe more with maths than with other subjects, the learner has to *believe* that he can do it or at the least make an attempt that will be genuinely valued. Self-concept, self-esteem, optimism and pessimism are concepts which we often discuss, but do we, as teachers keep them uppermost in our minds at all times? Sports managers pay big money to get their teams motivated and believing that they will win because they know how important those beliefs are to success, however skilled the team.

It's not what the child *can* do, it's what he *will* do that leads to success.

(John Hattie)[5]

8 The inconsistencies of maths

Consistency allows us a convenient, relatively effortless and efficient method for dealing with complex daily environments that make severe demands on our mental energies and capacities.

(Cialdini)[1]

Another general factor to consider for uncertain learners is inconsistency. This may be a change of teacher, a new topic, a different room or inconsistencies in the subject. This short chapter tries to help teachers and support assistants gain an extra understanding of this facet of maths and how it may confuse insecure pupils. As teachers of maths, we try to encourage pupils to look for patterns and this is generally sound practice, but then we must be aware of the confusions that may arise as a consequence of any exceptions. Unfortunately, many of the inconsistencies of maths occur in the very early topics with potential effects on the establishment of basic concepts.

When I first started teaching mathematics I would say to my students, 'Maths is much better than spelling because in maths a rule is a rule, no exceptions!' But if you teach pupils who have problems in learning maths you learn not to make assumptions and to question everything you might have taken for granted even, for example, the 'simple' process of counting to twenty (see below).

Inconsistencies will get in the way of generalising and pattern forming. Students with poor mathematical memories could use patterns and relationships to support their poor memory. If the patterns are disguised or have too any exceptions then the student has to commit more, seemingly unrelated, information to memory. It's the use of strategies based around patterns, relationships and understanding that supports learning.

The research reported by Hattie[2] found that, for maths, the programmes with the greatest effect on competency for LD and low achieving pupils were strategy-based methods.

I began to recognise two important elements in teaching maths to my pupils. One was that maths has far more inconsistencies than I realised[3] and the other was that students who find learning maths difficult need consistency and rely on consistency. Where there are inconsistencies then we as teachers have to be aware of them and help our students to manage them.

Then I thought about the interaction of pupils' confusions arising from these inconsistencies and some research from eighty years ago. Back in the 1920s two Americans, Buswell and Judd[4] wrote a monograph about teaching arithmetic. I have always felt that one of their observations is vitally important for learners (and teachers). Basically Buswell and Judd said that when you learn a new topic in arithmetic, if your first experience in practising and applying this new topic is incorrect, that inaccuracy becomes a dominant memory. So, for example, if despite careful teaching, the pupil adds $\frac{1}{20} + \frac{1}{20}$ as $\frac{2}{40}$, that procedural inaccuracy becomes what he remembers when faced with similar questions in future. Of course, if the learning experience is correct, then that stays, too.

So the inconsistencies of maths may lead to inaccurate and misleading first experiences. We as teachers have to be aware of this and try to pre-empt the confusion or at least check pupils' initial practice questions quickly before any misunderstanding becomes embedded in our learners' minds. To be more specific, we should not let students practice new work without checking the first few questions to ensure that what they are practicing is correct.

We need to monitor and utilise the power of the first learning experience.

There is also an issue with automaticity. When we can perform a task or recall information accurately and automatically then we can perform other tasks in addition. For example, when learning to drive a car, once changing gear becomes automatic we tend to steer better! In maths, when skills and tasks are automatic, other tasks are performed more accurately. For example, the most frequent error in computations, in all abilities, is the basic fact error. It's not that students don't know these facts when asked them separately, it's that they are less accurate when doing the other mental tasks involved in the computation.

Some of the inconsistencies which can create confusion for learners are listed below. Being aware of these may also aid diagnostic teaching. Confusion over inconsistencies may be the root of other problems as maths progresses.

The inconsistencies that may lead to future confusions in maths start in very early numeracy, for example and as already mentioned, in counting to twenty:

- We write numbers as 1, 2, 3, 4, 5, 6, 7, 8, 9, which are getting bigger as we write from left to right, then we write 11, 12, 13, 14, 15, 16, 17, 18, 19 where the bigger (value) digit is now on the left, even though it has been smaller in the earlier learning experience.
- The words for the first two-digit numbers, eleven and twelve, are exceptions. They are not part of any base ten vocabulary pattern.
- The words for the teen numbers defy the convention used for other two-digit numbers by referring to the unit digit first, thus thirteen compares badly with twenty-three, thirty-three and so on. Thus the vocabulary for the first two-digit numbers is contrary to any future pattern.
- While the language structure becomes regular for numbers in the hundreds and above using, for example five hundred, five thousand and five million, we use fifty, which is not only not fivety, but is not five ten. Fifty also sounds remarkably like fifteen. (Maybe this has something to do with the history of the language of maths and the lower frequency of use of the higher numbers giving less chance for them to become colloquial.)
- Children are likely to meet 'third' first (!) when used to denote order. Later the same word is used for a fraction.
- We have a whole range of words to infer addition, subtraction, multiplication and division. For example 'more, plus, and, add' all infer addition. So we can teach this flexibility in language and create classic maths word problems such as:

    Mark has eight pens. James has two more pens than Mark. How many pens does James have?

Then we use 'more' in a subtraction question:

    Mark has eight pens. Mark has two more pens than James. How many pens does James have?

(See also Chapter 6.)

- We used to use 'carry' in addition sums and 'decompose' in subtraction sums, yet both are trading actions, trading ten ones for one ten and trading one ten for ten ones. When I was at school (a long time ago) we used 'borrow and payback' for subtraction. It is better to have one word for what is essentially the same process. That also reinforces the link between the two operations.
- In early experiences of subtraction, it is tempting for teachers to tell pupils that we 'take the little from the big'. This does not remain a reliable concept. In setting up and marking the papers used for standardising the 15-minute screener test for *More Trouble with Maths*, this error was the most frequently occurring one for

$$\begin{array}{r} 33 \\ -16 \\ \hline 23 \end{array}$$

- Multiplying may be taught as a process that makes things bigger, yet multiplying by $\frac{1}{2}$, 10%, 0.6 and so forth makes things smaller. (Similar confusing things happen with division, where the assumption is that division makes things smaller.)
- We (normally) add, subtract and multiply in writing from units, through tens to hundreds and on, that is from right to left, but we divide from left to right and thus from thousands, to hundreds, tens and units. We may also add and subtract mentally starting from highest place value.
- We teach $7 \times 3 = 21$ for multiplication problems and then ask, 'How many threes in 22? Or 23? or 20? That is a significant extension of what was a simple concept. Also, the student has not linked 23 to 7 before.
- For numbers and algebra,

  a times b equals *b times a* ($ab = ba$) for example $3 \times 4 = 4 \times 3$

  a plus b equals *b plus a* ($a + b = b + a$) for example $3 + 4 = 4 + 3$

  but

  a divided by b does not equal *b divided by a* ($a/b \neq b/a$) for example $\frac{2}{3} \neq \frac{3}{2}$

  a minus b does not equal *b minus a* ($a - b \neq b - a$)

  for example $2 - 3 \neq 3 - 2$

- We expect absolute accuracy in numerical computations and then expect students to abandon this strict regime when learning to estimate.
- We teach place value and say 3456 as 'three thousand, four hundred and fifty-six' but a pupil may also experience a four-digit number as a year, for example, 1980, which we say as 'nineteen eighty' or 1066, which we say as 'ten sixty-six'
- In fractions, the most familiar (and therefore the most useful, potentially, for teaching) are the three inconsistently named fractions, half, third and quarter. The rest, a fifth, sixth and so on are OK.
- In fractions, big becomes small. For example, $\frac{1}{9}$ is smaller than $\frac{1}{2}$.
- Again, in fractions, we modify the use of the addition sign so, for example in

$$\frac{1}{5} + \frac{3}{5} = \frac{4}{5}$$

only the 'top' numbers are added. The + symbol only operates on half of the numbers. Then we change again so that in multiplications such as

$$\frac{2}{5} \times \frac{3}{5} = \frac{6}{25}$$

both 'top' and 'bottom' numbers are multiplied. The $\times$ symbol operates on both numbers in the fraction.

- In whole numbers the sequence of words for the place values going from left to right of the decimal point is units, tens, hundreds, thousands. For decimals, the sequence from right to left of the decimal point is tenths, hundredths, thousandths, which is a very subtle difference in sounds, but a big difference in concept:

    5382.739

    One 3 is 'three hundreds' and the other is 'three hundredths'. The 'ths' are almost silent.

- If learners focus on the decimal point, which is very tempting, then there is a loss of symmetry. The whole number sequence is units, tens, hundreds, thousands. The decimal sequence is tenths, hundredths, thousandths. There is no uniths (of course). The focus and the symmetry are around 'units' not around the decimal point.

- With angles we tend to measure anti-clockwise, but with time we work clockwise.

- There are 90° in a right angle (would 100° cause fewer problems?), and what about a campaign to change the 12 hours for a half day to 10 (just joking, don't tell the EC).

Base ten is rooted in counting the ten digits we have on our hands. Base twelve is rooted in the number of segments on four fingers, with the thumb used as the counter.

- Time works with 12 and 60 instead of 10 and 100 and is cyclical, that is we count up to 12 (sometimes 24 to add more confusion) and 60 and then start at 1 again. We do this with days (in 7s) and months (in 12s) too and weeks are in 52s.

- With time we count on from the hour until half past, then we count down to the next hour. So 4:30 is 'four thirty', but 4:40 is 'twenty to five' (4:40 having neither a twenty nor a five)

- 7:10 can be verbalised as 'Seven ten', which has the words in the same order as the numbers, or as 'Ten past seven', which has the words in reverse order.

- The basic unit of length is the metre, m. The basic unit of volume is the litre, l. The basic unit of mass is the kilogram, kg, not the gram, g.

- In measurement 'm' means metre, mile and milli (but not mega and micro)

- Children are often told that multiplying a number by 1 does not change the number, yet in fractions, for example

    $$\frac{2}{3} \times \frac{5}{5} = \frac{10}{15}$$

    $\frac{10}{15}$ is the same *value* as $\frac{2}{3}$ but certainly does not look the same.

- In algebra we use x to mean 'any number'. Then we give pupils $3x + 8 = 20$, and ask them to find a particular number value for x.

- And in arithmetic $\times$ has always meant multiply, now in algebra it doesn't, and further than this, in algebra we omit any symbol for multiply.

- In algebra we can represent 'multiply' as $w(y + 6)$ or as ab or as b^2, but we do not represent multiplication with $\times$.

- In algebra we keep the symbols $+$ and $-$ but lose $\times$ and $\div$.

- 'Remove the brackets' as in $(y + 3)(y - 5)$ is not meant literally. Neither is 'Find x'. Neither is 'expand'.

- In calculus the dy (and dx) in $\frac{dy}{dx}$ does not mean d times y and d times x.

- In trigonometry $\sin^{-1}$ does not mean 1/sin.

This list covers a few key examples. As time goes by and I teach each new class, I learn new things and I continue to add to my list of inconsistencies. My students continue to teach me about understanding maths. Teaching is always about learning.

When he was a young man, the Nobel Prize winning scientist Richard Feynman invented his own symbols for trigonometry, calculus and other areas of maths, which were to him far more consistent than the traditional symbols (for example in $\frac{dx}{dy}$ he was tempted to cancel the '*d*'s). Unfortunately, reality intervened and he realised that to communicate with other mathematicians he had to use the same symbols as they did. So I guess reality will have to rule here, too and we will have to accept and work with the inconsistencies. We have to teach children and adults to deal with these inconsistencies. To do that we have to be aware that they exist.

Just to complete the chapter I have reproduced an article I wrote, obviously written very tongue in cheek, published originally in *Mathematics Teaching*, a journal of the Association of Teachers of Mathematics (ATM). It is reprinted with ATM permission.

It was just a matter of time[5]

Old Dr Algy B'rah faced the Lower 3rd maths class for lesson 10 on Friday afternoon.

'Now, today, or perhaps it was yesterday, when I said it would be tomorrow. In fact sometime recently I said that it was about time I spent some time teaching you time.

Time is easy to understand and to help I've brought in a real clock. This is the clock face. You'll see that it doesn't have eyes or a nose but it does have hands. Unlike you there are three hands to one face. The first hand is the hour hand, the second hand is the minute hand and the third hand is the second hand. Is that clear?

The little hand is the hour hand and the big hand is the minute hand. That's minute not minute, otherwise it wouldn't be big would it?

There are numbers round the clock face. They start with 1, which is not the number at the top, and go round to 12, which is at the top. This is because there are 24 hours in a day. So there are 24 hours in a day and we put 12 of them on a clock and use them twice.

See all these little marks. They are the marks for minutes, which can also be used for seconds and there are 60 of those, so 1 means 1 if it's hours and 5 if it's minutes and 5 if its seconds and 2 means 10 minutes when it's not hours and 10 seconds when it's not minutes. So there are 60 minutes in an hour and 60 seconds in a minute and we only use them once, not twice like hours.

When the big hand is pointing at 12 and the little hand is pointing at 4 it is four o'clock. No it isn't really 4 o'clock now, sit down, and no, Seamus, o'clock is not an Irish name.

The hands go round and round and round. It is all very logical. It takes the hour hand $\frac{1}{2}$ day to go round. It takes the minute hand an hour to go round and it takes the second hand a minute to go round. And when the hour hand has been round twice it's tomorrow and today becomes yesterday.

Now, when we start to go past o'clock, we get to times like 5 past 1, which we write as 1.05. This means the little hand starts to move away from the 1 and the minute hand moves away from the 12. The little hand heads for 2 and the big, minute hand moves away from the 12, which also means zero, but it doesn't say it, and heads for the 1, which also means 5. This goes until 30 past 1, which is also half past 1, which is also 1.30, but the . is not a decimal and 30 is not the decimal .30, which is $\frac{3}{10}$ but now it's $\frac{1}{2}$, not .50 so we have to remember that $\frac{1}{2}$ can be written as .30, but if you do that with decimal numbers I will mark it wrong. Then we say 25 to 2, which is not tutu or to to or two two and 20 to 2 and quarter to 2 and 10 to 2. Of course 20 to 2 could be one third to 2, but that would be difficult so we don't say that, because we want time to be easy. And of course 20 to 2 could be one forty, which is not the same as forty one backwards, because we always say the hour first except when we say it second after the minutes. And the to is not two or 10 to 2 would be 1022, which is forty-four years before the Battle of Hastings.

So we count in minutes after the hour, but only until 30 minutes after the hour, then we count down to the next hour, even though the minute hand is now moving up, except when we use times like 1.35. This means we change the hour we are talking about at half past the first hour and use the next hour half an hour before we reach the next hour. Once you think about that it all becomes clear, doesn't it?

Now you have all that clear we can move on to the 24 hour clock, which is used for trains, buses and aeroplanes, all examples where you really need to know time to be on time. We still use the 12 hour clock face I've shown you but when we go round the second time with the hour hand we now have to remember that for the 24 hour clock 1 means 13, 2 is 14, 3 is 15 and so on. So the 1 on the clock face can mean 1 for hours, 13 for hours, 5 for minutes and 5 for seconds. When we get past 6 numbers like 9 can mean 9, 21, 45 or $\frac{1}{4}$ and 7 can mean 7, 19, 35 or 25. And don't forget that $10 + 5 = 3$ with the 12 hour clock and $10 + 5 = 15$ with the 24 hour clock and $23 + 8 = 07$ with the 24 hour clock and I know we haven't written 0 in front of a whole number before.

On the 24 hour clock after times like fifteen fifty-nine we go to sixteen hundred, which is really fifteen sixty, but after 59 we go back to zero again and call it hundred. This means we have to remember that 20.40 is not the same as 20.40 in decimals but is the same as 8.40 and 20 to 9. That's clear to me, so it should be clear to you.

I just can't understand why you can't do time. No I don't mean "do time" as in "doing time" Bodger.'

And we expect young children to understand time!

Learners who are insecure or uncertain do not handle inconsistencies well. Time is full of inconsistencies, in the vocabulary used and in the way numbers are used.

9 Manipulatives and materials: multisensory learning

Why use manipulatives and materials?

It seems strange to me that as maths progresses to ever more complex concepts that, in many classrooms, materials and manipulatives are no longer used. Somewhere, sometime in the history of maths most of these materials became associated with young children and the early stages and concepts of maths. Maybe that was because some materials look childish. Maybe that it is down to the bright, primary colours used with many materials.

Maybe another reason is that many materials make sense to teachers, but not to children. For example, Dearden, back in 1967 when much of education was about children discovering for themselves, observed:

> When a teacher presents a child with some apparatus or materials, he typically has in mind some particular conception of what he presents in this way.
>
> But then the incredible assumption seems to be made that the teacher's conception of the situation somehow confers a special uniqueness on it such that the children must also quite inevitably conceive of it in this way too.[1]

and Kath Hart in 1989 noted:

> When asked for the connection between practical work and the symbolic statement of a rule, the children's best reply was that one was a quicker route to the answer than the other.[2]

It may also be that materials are used for topics for which they are not suitable. Different materials have different characteristics and those characteristics often relate to specific language and to specific concepts.

Some would have us believe that materials are a panacea. Again, 'it's a little more complicated than that'.

Often with materials it's a matter of 'horses for courses', a matter of selecting the material that is most appropriate for the concept and the learner. That's why maths rooms need a wide range of resources.

In Chapter 5, I explained the developmental nature of maths. The development is about topics, how we progress from counting to adding and multiplying, to fractions, to algebra. But the development is also about understanding concepts, not just about becoming a more sophisticated calculating machine. Unfortunately human calculating machines are likely to forget their functions!

In that early stage of maths, counting, it is likely that we will count on our fingers or on objects. The objects may be things that we can touch and move, or drawings on paper that we can touch and see. It takes a while for us to learn how to count 'in our heads', without using objects and pictures. That shift seems to me to be quite a challenge.

Butterworth considers that the skill of subitising, being able to look at a (small) number of objects and know how many are there, is a prerequisite skill for learning maths. Subitising is about relating a visual image to a number that represents the quantity. So, at this fundamental stage, the skill is related to objects, seeing them, appraising the number, naming the number of objects.

Butterworth's other prerequisite is 'numerical stroop'. Essentially this is about recognising the values that digit symbols represent, knowing with security, for example that 8 is bigger than 3, even if the 8 is presented in a smaller font than the 3.

This skill is about securely and accurately identifying the symbols we use to represent quantity. There is no material or visual support in this sub-test (and not meant to be). It is about symbols.

These skills are so fundamental it would be hard to disagree with their place in Butterworth's model. Number sense has to start somewhere. However, subsequent developments from these basics have a crucial role to play. These subsequent skills, usually skills that are taught, are the next level in the maths knowledge and skill wall.

The fundamental skills, including subitising and digit recognition, are often taught (or should be) using materials, manipulatives, objects, images, something we can touch and see. I cannot imagine that we would conceive of it being learned, or taught, in any other way.

Because the knowledge that is being developed is so fundamental to the future learning of maths, it should be taught extremely carefully and knowledgeably, using appropriate images, appropriate language and vocabulary.

I was looking at a beautifully designed children's book for the first ten numbers. It was elegant, attractive and illustrated with clear, imaginative images. However, throughout the book the pictures were randomly presented and in the summary at the end the dots for each number were presented in a line. Patterns were not used. Presenting ten dots in a line tends to encourage counting in ones. It is not just the material or the image, but the way it is constructed and presented to show 'maths'. Concepts begin to develop even at this earliest of stages. A child may be able to do the counting, but this could be an early example of the illusion of learning. Knowing the counting sequence does not automatically confer understanding (and number sense).

When used appropriately, materials encourage the recognition of patterns and connections. In this way they can support long-term memory. That is one of their key roles, but there is another key role, the role of assisting in the development of concepts. The materials do not have to be complex or expensive, just effective.

If we want children (and adults) to understand maths we should actively acknowledge the cognitive developmental stages by structuring our explanations accordingly. So, my hypothesis is that we have to relate topic to topic, to build on acquired knowledge and to illustrate, literally, each new topic. It's called 'understanding'!

Jean Piaget explained the stages of development of cognitive attainment. The concrete stage, the stage when the learner needs materials, and the pictorial stage are precursors for the abstract and symbolic stages. Materials set the basis for higher levels of understanding.

Can students take a new view?

There is another possible benefit in using materials here. Buswell and Judd's observations from over eighty years ago, that what we learn when we first meet a new topic or new knowledge is a dominant entry to our brain, may explain why it is so difficult to retrain the bad maths habits and incorrect knowledge that some children acquire. The use of materials may present the information in a new form and may be a better way of addressing erroneous knowledge than simply trying to practise using a minor variation of the first method of instruction or, worse still, practising what they can't do. We know as adults that what we learned about maths at school tends to re-emerge when we are trying to do maths under stress.

Multisensory

When explaining a new topic or a new concept we use both general vocabulary and vocabulary that is specific to the topic (see Chapter 6) in order to communicate, to explain. But we may also need visual input. If I move away from maths for a moment and think about what we expect from a Sat Nav. We expect that we will be given information orally and visually. We expect to receive information in both modes and we know that this means that the information is received more clearly as a result.

But again, as science writer Ben Goldacre says, 'I think you'll find that it's a little more complicated than that.' Unfortunately, I cannot track down the source, but someone who is very wise said, 'Materials do not teach. Teachers teach.' The point being made is that materials may be a good idea, but they cannot work alone, they need to be used by a skilled teacher who knows what they are supposed to illustrate and why they are appropriate for that purpose. And they have to mean the same to the learner. The teacher has to mediate and communicate.

There are many materials that are produced commercially for teaching maths. There are even more that are not commercially produced, just everyday objects, but are out there, waiting for a creative teacher to use them. Once more it is about collecting resources (and knowing how to use them).

An example: this shows an interaction, or even an interdependence between the materials and the language (see Figure 9.1).

The numbers and symbols are:

$$7 - 4 = 3$$

The language chosen is:

'Seven take away four' and 'What is the difference between seven and four?'

For 'Seven take away four' I have chosen counters. It could have been 1p coins. For 'What is the difference?' I have chosen Stern blocks or their modern equivalent, Numicon shapes.

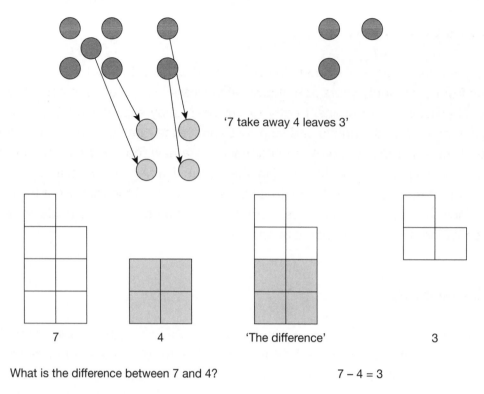

'7 take away 4 leaves 3'

7   4   'The difference'   3

What is the difference between 7 and 4?   7 – 4 = 3

Figure 9.1 Subtraction and language

Moving on from counting in ones: which materials help?

Counting in ones is where it begins, but not where it should stay. Which materials can help cognitive growth best? What are the characteristics of the materials that illustrate the concept? And is 'the best material', the best for all learners?

Counters . . . I do like the chunky poker chips . . . very tactile . . . they could, as might any discrete material, keep the learner working in ones, unless we use the counters/chips in consistent and recognisable patterned groups. The patterns below should help the learner to recognise number values beyond 1 without drawing on subitising skills for random clusters. The patterns also help to link the numbers, for example, 9 is one less than 10, 10 is one more than 9, 5 is half of 10, double 5 is 10. The counters are flexible in the number values they can represent.

Counting beyond 10 and place value

Place value is a very sophisticated concept. It introduces zero, another sophisticated concept. Zero is likely to cause more errors in future maths than any other digit. Because place value is part of everyday counting and number work, we may overlook its complexity and influence. (See the sheep counters in Chapter 5 and Figure 5.1.)

If we wanted to work with numbers beyond 10, we could introduce a colour scheme for the counters for units and tens. So, for example, blue counters could be chosen to represent units and red counters represent tens. The learner has to know, with automaticity, that the colour relates to place value. A ten counter is not ten times bigger than a one counter. This is a move to the symbolic stage. That may be a quantum leap for some learners. In such cases it may be that the next move is to base ten (Dienes) blocks where the 10 block looks (because it is!) ten times as big as a 1 block.

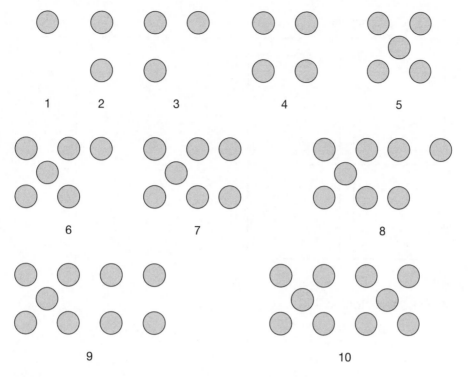

Figure 9.2 Patterns for 1 to 10

So, base ten blocks are proportional in size to the number values they represent. A ten 'long' is the same size as ten unit cubes lined up. A one hundred square or 'flat' is the same size as ten 'longs' placed side by side. Learners can check this by handling the blocks or the images can be manipulated on an interactive white board. Thus the blocks can be used to demonstrate place value. The longs are visually ten times longer than a unit cube, the one hundred flat is ten times bigger than one long block.

Students who like tactile materials may need the blocks to be made from wood so that the bigger blocks feel proportionately heavier.

You can illustrate 45 with 4 ten blocks and 5 unit cubes, as shown in Figure 9.3. And 405 can be illustrated with 4 one hundred flats and 5 unit cubes (see Figure 9.4). The absence of any ten blocks in this illustration demonstrates that there are zero ten blocks. Placing the blocks on a place value card may enhance this demonstration.

So we have 400 in one hundred blocks and 5 in unit cubes . . . 400 + 5 = 405 . . . the tens place has zero blocks and thus this is represented as 0 in the number 405.

What makes base ten blocks applicable to so many early concepts is that they reinforce the role of place value.

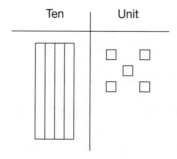

Figure 9.3 Base ten blocks: 45

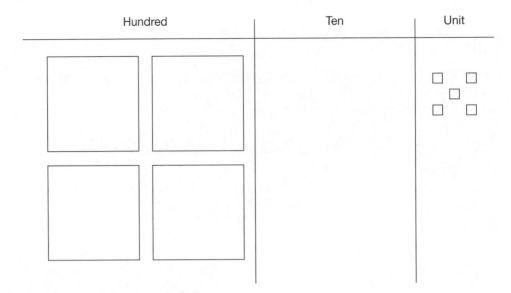

Figure 9.4 Base ten blocks: 405

Counting on units, tens and hundreds

The blocks can be used to demonstrate that adding units does not change the tens until ten units are reached, adding tens does not change the units, adding hundreds does not change the tens or the units.

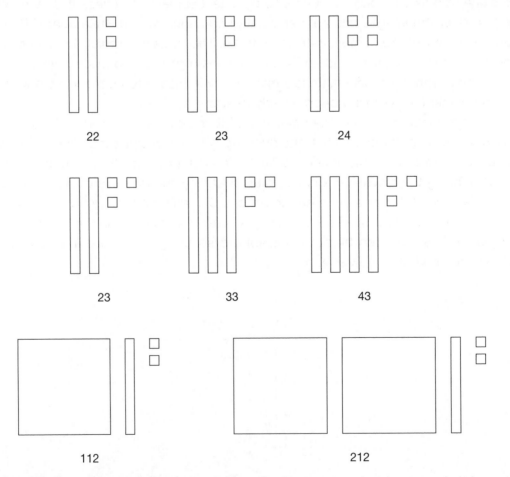

Figure 9.5 Counting on units, tens and hundreds

There are other materials that can be used to illustrate these actions and concepts. For example, adding in tens can also be demonstrated with a one hundred bead string. If each child has their own bead string then the teacher can ask the class to hold up their string and show their answer and thus monitor the success of each pupil.

It is possible to work with Stern or Numicon blocks but, once again, ensuring that the recognition of the ten block is automatic.

Coins can be used to illustrate decimal values, but, yet again, it is important to ensure that the pupils confidently and automatically recognise the values of the two coins, the 10p coin and the 1p coin and relate them to 0.1 and 0.01. Using coins also takes the maths into everyday life.

Coins are not proportional to the values they represent. A ten pence coin is not ten times bigger that a one-pence coin. The learner has to be automatic in their recognition of the values each coin represents or the coins will not illustrate the processes.

Base ten blocks can also be used to illustrate decimal number values, and down to thousandths, but this does challenge the consistency principle ... the learner has to accept that what was once a thousand cube is now being used to represent one unit. Perhaps this makes an argument for having a set of 'decimal' cubes in different colours?

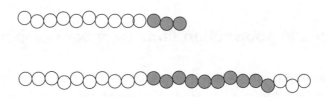

Figure 9.6 Bead string: 13 and 23

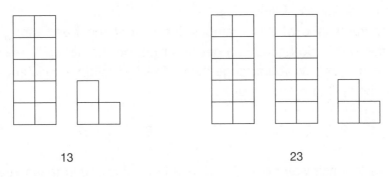

13   23

Figure 9.7 Stern and Numicon blocks: 13 and 23

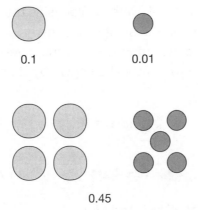

0.1   0.01

0.45

Figure 9.8 Coins and decimals

The base ten materials also lead to illustrations of very large numbers, to the pattern of 1000s that we use for millions, billions and trillions. For example, 10 to 100 to 1000 is 'long', 'square', 'cube', ending up with a 10cm-sided cube. 10,000 to 1,000,000 is also 'long', 'square', 'cube', ending up with a 1m-sided cube.

The three-dimensional properties of the base ten materials lead to a very different image of the large numbers, for example, a billion, than does a linear image. Both have to be imagined, so these are imaginary visuals, although we can provide a yardstick image to give reality to the concept.

If we take 1mm as the unit, then a metre is 1000 and a kilometre is a million (1000 times 1000). A thousand kilometres will be one thousand million millimetres, a billion. To put this into a UK distance perspective, from Truro to Aberdeen by car is a drive of 1080 kilometres.

If we consider the unit cube of the base ten materials to be one, then the 10cm (decimetre) cube is one thousand. A million one centimetre cubes will fit into a cube of sides one metre. A billion unit cubes would fit into a cube with sides of ten metres. And a trillion?

These images give some realisation to numbers that are so big they are almost unimaginable.

Basic addition and subtraction facts (number combinations)

In Chapter 3, I discussed which are the key basic addition facts to learn, so for the following examples I will focus on the number bonds for 10 and the doubles.

The number bonds for 10 can be illustrated with a number of materials, for example, a bead string, Cuisenaire rods and counters. Let's start with the bead string, a bead string showing two groups of five.

The first characteristic of this manipulative is that the bead string emphasises the conservation of 10. No beads can get on or get off the string. There must always be 10 beads no matter how you arrange them. The illustration then is about how those ten beads can be split into two groups . . .

$$0 + 10 \qquad 1 + 9 \qquad 2 + 8 \qquad 3 + 7 \qquad 4 + 6 \qquad 5 + 5$$

. . . which is the key half way point. 5 + 5 is a key value within these key values. The dialogue that accompanies the visual images could consider how one group of beads gets one smaller each time as the other gets one larger (with the total always being 10).

The learner needs to see the digit symbols alongside the beads to help the connection between the concrete stage and the symbolic stage.

At the half way point the beads start to show the reverse pattern. The commutative property, for example, 7 + 3 = 3 + 7 can be shown by simply turning the beads around.

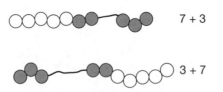

Figure 9.9 Bead string for number bonds for 10

The colouring of the beads in groups of five should help the learner to group rather than count in ones. This should be demonstrated and practised. It should not be assumed that a learner will automatically pick up the pattern.

This demonstration can be developed further. For example, for an illustration that takes the idea of $7 + ? = 10$ to $7 + x = 10$ we can hide three beads, show the 7 and ask, 'How many beads to make ten?' If the bead string is coloured to show two groups of 5, then this may link the visual image to the counter pattern shown in Figure 9.9 and the concept of relating other numbers to the key numbers, 1, 2, 5 and 10. So, we have two visual images to use, one that is visible, one that is hidden. Since both are working on the same number structure, the two visuals could be discussed simultaneously. The answer is 3. Now the question is, 'Is that action related in the learner's mind to and connected with the symbolic representations $7 + ? = 10$ or $7 + \square = 10$ or $7 + y = 10$? This connection may well need an explicit explanation. This seemingly simple three stage development takes the learner from numbers and a bead string to algebra and links addition and subtraction. If the learner cannot understand $7 + y = 10$, then understanding the development allows the teacher to track back to find the level at which the learner is secure and then to discuss the stage and its implications.

All the presentations relate subtraction to adding on. They are demonstrating $10 - 7$ by asking, 'What do I add on to 7 to make 10?' The cognitive demands that can be extracted from this illustration can be varied from adding on for subtraction to algebra. Indeed, later in the curriculum, the explanation of the algebra might well start with a return to the number demonstration.

One of the themes running through this book, although not always implicitly is, 'What else are you teaching?'

The next materials I want to consider are Cuisenaire rods. These are not discrete. There are no markings to count. The lengths are related, but not defined. If the smallest rod is specified to be one, then the biggest rod will be ten. If the smallest rod is defined as one hundred, then the shaded rod will be one thousand. Cuisenaire rods are good for illustrating, 'Is it bigger or smaller?' They are also good for taking the learner to generalisations and patterns. Since you cannot count to find out the value, you have to take a holistic view.

For example, the number bonds for 10 and 100 and 1000 and 1.0 are all represented by the arrangement shown in Figure 9.10, which clearly shows that in each pair of consecutive rods, one gets smaller as the other gets bigger and that the pattern repeats in the opposite sequence after $5 + 5$ (or $0.5 + 0.5$ or $50 + 50$ or $500 + 500$). That bigger/smaller concept may be all you want to demonstrate with these materials. Cuisenaire rods help with the general picture, the estimate, the overview and often the patterns and generalisations.

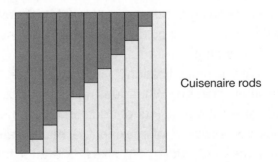

Cuisenaire rods

Figure 9.10 Images of number bonds for 1, 10, 100, 1000

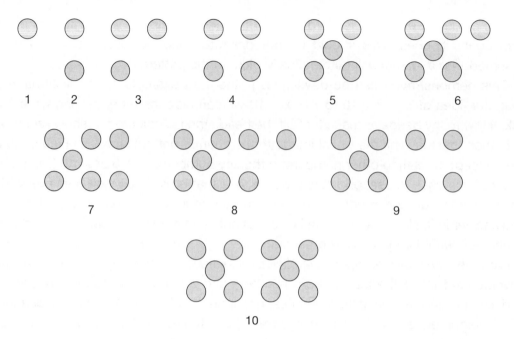

Figure 9.11 Counters (or coins) in a consistent and interrelating pattern

The third and final example uses counters (or coins) that are set out in the familiar and consistent and inter-relating pattern.

Basic multiplication and division facts (number combinations)

There are a number of underlying concepts that should make these facts understandable. The persistence of the belief that rote learning these facts is some magic foundation for being good at maths is stunning. There is nothing wrong with rote learning these facts, if you can, but there is something wrong with not understanding them.

To make a point, I had to try and learn the twelve times facts when I was a child, because England was still using Imperial measures. I was educated in the pre-decimal era. Why would I want to learn the twelve times facts nowadays? Even egg cartons, the last bastion of dozens, are being replaced with cartons holding ten eggs. I recently met a German man, my sort of age, who told me that he had to learn up to his twenty-one times tables at school. Useful if ever they decide to sell eggs in boxes of nineteen.

A times tables (or multiplication) fact is called a fact because you are supposed to remember it, retrieve it from memory, not work it out. But, by not learning how to work out these facts by methods other than counting, children are missing out on some key concepts and some basic building blocks of mathematics. In other words, even if the student can rote-learn the facts, they should still be shown how the facts are constructed. Which is where the materials come in.

If you ask students, 'What is multiplication?' you may well get the answer, 'Repeated addition'. The next question could be, 'What does repeated addition mean?' It does not mean doing a long worksheet that has lots of addition problems.

Multiplication is another example of making the manipulation of numbers more efficient. For example, instead of adding ten sixes, one after the other, we do this in one operation, multiplication, $6 \times 10 = 60$.

Cuisenaire rods can be used to illustrate the concept of multiplication as repeated addition. As ever the digits should be presented alongside the materials.

For example,

6 × 5

One 5 rod can be shown alongside the symbols 1 × 5 (children can be confused about 1×). It may be necessary to explain the language, to translate maths–English to English–English, linking 'one lot of 5', which can be modelled, to 'one times 5', which cannot be modelled.

Then, for example, five 5 rods, alongside each other, 5 + 5 + 5 + 5 + 5 and 5 × 5 and more explanation of the language and the emerging area model. The importance of 5× facts as key facts can be discussed. The simple reason behind 'key fact' status is that these facts tend to be remembered or readily accessed and extended.

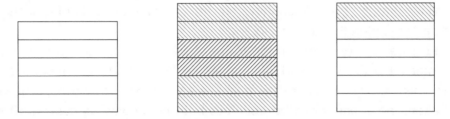

Figure 9.12 Cuisenaire rods for 5 × 5 and (2 × 5) + (2 × 5) + (2 × 5) and (5 × 5) + (1 × 5)

The demonstration should build to 6 × 5. The rods can be discussed and re-arranged to show various combinations and, as ever, linked to the symbols.

For example, 5 + 5 + 5 + 5 + 5 + 5

And   (5 + 5) + (5 + 5) + (5 + 5)

And   2 × 5 + 2 × 5 + 2 × 5

And   (5 + 5 + 5 + 5 + 5) + (5)

And   (5 × 5) + (5)

In all these demonstrations the concept of partial products is being developed. Related to this is the linking of key facts to access other facts.

The conceptual learning demonstrated here sets the foundation for future topics, for example, 'long' multiplication and in collecting like terms used in algebra. Again the point is that children who simply rote learn these facts may miss out on understanding how they work and how they relate to those future topics. I can extend this argument by suggesting that in helping the children who find rote learning problematic you help the other children too.

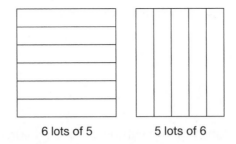

6 lots of 5   5 lots of 6

Figure 9.13 Cuisenaire rods and the commutative property

The commutative property for multiplication, for example, 5 × 6 = 6 × 5, or in algebra, $a \times b = b \times a$, $ab = ba$, virtually halves the number of basic facts you need to learn. It is also of use in algebra.

Cuisenaire rods can be used for an effective demonstration of this property. By setting out and talking through the relationships, several commutative sets of Cuisenaire rods, it can be demonstrated that $a \times b = b \times a$

Squared paper can do a similar job to the Cuisenaire rods, but presenting a more symbolic image. For the 6 × 5 and 5 × 6 example, two rectangles are cut out for these facts and then shown to have the same area, as with the rods, but with this demonstration, the squares can be counted, both rectangles containing 30 squares. The Cuisenaire rod demonstration is more grasshopper, that is, it illustrates the idea that the two arrays are the same. The squared paper is more inchworm in that it allows the learner to count the squares to prove they are the same area, because they both have 30 squares. The rods can be used to present several examples and thus encourage generalising as a precursor to understanding the algebra.

The strategies for working out all the basic facts (and many more beyond that collection) are discussed in Chapter 5, but I will just take the two Cuisenaire rod illustrations from above and extend them to demonstrate the partial products route to finding multiplication 'facts'.

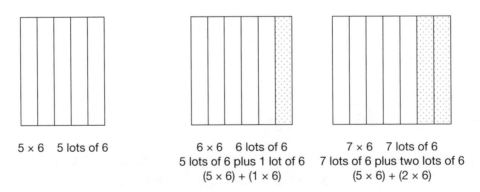

5 × 6   5 lots of 6

6 × 6   6 lots of 6
5 lots of 6 plus 1 lot of 6
(5 × 6) + (1 × 6)

7 × 6   7 lots of 6
7 lots of 6 plus two lots of 6
(5 × 6) + (2 × 6)

Figure 9.14 Cuisenaire rods and building facts

Number lines

A number line is a basic material, certainly in terms of cost. You can use a 'full' number line or an 'empty' number line. A rule is a ready made number line. A metre rule could be used to illustrate tenths, hundredths and thousandths as well as zero to 1000 and multiplying and dividing by 10, 100 and 1000.

Conceptually there is a difference between an empty number line, which encourages estimation, and a full number line which encourages counting (hopefully not always in ones). Since the empty number line encourages estimation skills it can also be presented as a tool which is less judgemental. Answers can be 'close' or 'maybe you could get a bit closer'.

It is not necessary to build a whole lesson around one manipulative. It could be used to illustrate one idea and, even then, may not be the only visual used.

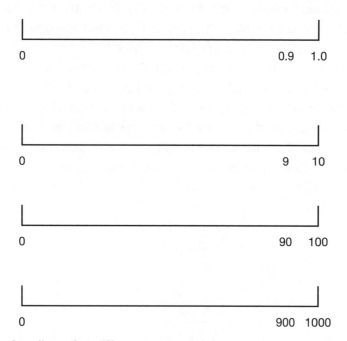

Figure 9.15 Number lines for different powers of ten

The personal white (wipe-clean) board

I'm not really sure that this is a material. It doesn't illustrate any concept or process, yet I feel that it has a vital place in the toolbox or resources cupboard. I have mentioned, more than once, the researchers who have observed the situation where children do not connect the materials to the numbers and the concept. There is a need for the learner to write the symbols as they use the materials. A white board may encourage this.

A key reason for using a personal whiteboard is risk-taking. The writing on the board can be wiped clean. There is no evidence of any error. Whiteboards can, therefore, encourage involvement.

Interactive whiteboards and computer programs

The same principles that apply to real materials apply to virtual materials! There are some remarkable resources for interactive whiteboards (for example, see the 'NLVM' from the USA and 'nzmaths' from New Zealand).

A caution here is with regard to the design of visuals. My rule is to 'keep it simple'. Over-fussy graphics will confuse some learners. Over-design can detract from the message.

Paper

From high-tech to low-tech! Paper, and drawings on paper, can be powerful teaching tools. For example, paper folding can illustrate fractions.

The principle of equivalent fractions and why fractions have to have the same denominator can be demonstrated with paper. Built into this is a demonstration of actions such as 'a third of a half' and the commutative 'a half of a third'.

Figure 9.16 shows a rectangle of paper folded to show a half.

Figure 9.17 shows the same size rectangle folded to show a third.

The half and the third are not the same size and thus cannot be combined.

Figure 9.18 shows the 'half' paper folded into thirds and the 'third' paper folded into halves. The resulting sixths are, of course the same size and thus it is possible to add a third and a half if both are converted to sixths. (This is a version of $2 \times 3 = 3 \times 2$ or $\div\ 3 \div 2 = \div 2 \div 3$.) One half becomes 3 sixths. One third becomes 2 sixths. The addition gives 5 sixths.

Figure 9.16 Folding to make a half

Figure 9.17 Folding to make a third

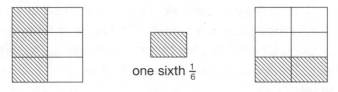

one sixth $\frac{1}{6}$

Figure 9.18 The 'half' paper folded into thirds and the 'third' paper folded into halves – both create sixths

The demonstration also shows that multiplying a fraction that is less than 1 by another fraction less than 1 results in a fraction that is smaller than either original fraction. In this case:

$\frac{1}{2} \times \frac{1}{3} = \frac{1}{6}$

The Singapore Model Method (see also Chapter 6)[3]

In 2009 Singapore came second in the PISA results for maths. The UK came twenty-eighth.

The 1982 Cockcroft Report (UK) into the teaching of mathematics in schools inspired the Singapore government to improve its students' abilities to problem solve. The UK didn't seem to achieve the same improvements.

The Singapore Model Method has created significant success for students. There will always be the caution that, however good a method is it will not work for everyone. There are a number of reasons why I consider this is so successful.

- It is low cost!
- It is developmental from a Piagetian perspective.
- It is consistent.
- The illustrations clarify. Many illustrations used in maths confuse.
- It encourages analysis and reflection.

A few illustrations.

The method moves from drawing pictures in Primary One, for example:

'Mark has three toy cars'

To a pictorial model

3

Or a more representative model

3

There is a consideration of 'Is it bigger or smaller?' for example:

'Mark has two more toys than James. Mark has ten toys. How many toys does James have?'

Mark

| | Mark has more toys (bigger) |

James

| | James has less toys (smaller) |

10 toys

| |

| | ← 2 toys → |

Thus James has 10 − 2 = 8 toys

The method is widely applicable, for example:

'Sam has 30 toy cars. He has 6 times as many toy cars as Pete. How many toy cars does Pete have?'

Pete | | (algebra *n* toy cars)

Sam has six times as many toy cars

Sam | | | | | | | (algebra 6*n* toy cars)

So, Pete's rectangle/model represents 5 toy cars.
Sam's model shows six times as many. Thus 6 × 5 = 30

Characteristics of materials

By now you will have read about different materials being used for developing different concepts. Some materials do a better job with some concepts than others. Classrooms need a selection of materials, some ready-made and some created by the teacher. In the Department of Education's (UK) DVD on using materials there are some wonderful examples of commercially available materials in use and also some creative uses of other equipment such as a metal money box that clunks every time a coin is dropped in it. And it makes a different clunk for one-pence coins and for ten pence coins. That example is one of the few materials I have seen that utilises the auditory mode to support learning. Another on the same DVD are some 'croaking frogs', little metal frogs that click when you press them, that are hanging from a coat hanger. Another visual and auditory material.

Some materials encourage counting in ones (discrete materials), for example, counters and bead strings, but they can also be clustered to encourage counting in groups (see Figure 9.2).

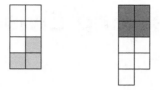

Figure 9.19 'Odd (5) plus odd (3) makes even (8)' and 'odd (5) plus even (4) makes odd (9)'

Base ten blocks are, of course, ideal for teaching base ten.

Some materials require the learner to be able to estimate values, for example an empty number line or Cuisenaire rods.

The Stern blocks (and the Numicon version) do a very good job on illustrating the properties of 'odd plus odd makes an even' and 'odd plus even makes an odd'.

I speculate that the digital watch more closely matches the inchworm learner (see Chapter 4) and the analogue watch the grasshopper learner. The digital watch gives you the time as digits that can be read without any need for understanding. This is a literal interpretation of time. The analogue watch requires the user to understand the concept of time, for example the 12 hours on the clock face, the 60 minutes and how they relate to each other.

I hope that this chapter makes a strong argument for having a resource base for materials, even if it is only a cupboard. The materials need to be on hand for regular use and to deal with those moments when a concept needs an appropriate (extra) illustration.

It's a three-way relationship: the material, the concept, the learner. If they all match then there is a strong chance that learning will take place.

Final point: the maths toolbox

Sue Clarkson and Maxine Slade from the Francis Baily Primary School, Berkshire, suggest the use of a maths tool box. DIY stores sell tool boxes of various sizes which share the same characteristic. They look 'grown up', the kind of box an adult would use. By using such toolboxes the image of the manipulatives placed inside them may be perceived as less childish. This image can be further enhanced by putting in other maths equipment such as a calculator, a compass, set square, protractor and mirror (for work on symmetry). The boxes could be left, readily available, in the classroom so that the pupil can take a box when he needs some of the contents. It is also about developing this as a natural part of the ethos of that classroom for all pupils.

More information

Paul Swan and Geoff White, from Western Australia, have written an excellent series of books on using manipulative materials, entitled *Hands-on Maths.*[4]

10 The nasties: long division and fractions

To illustrate some ideas and principles for teaching maths topics I have picked long division and fractions. I would guess that the two leading contenders for the most anxiety inducing, no attempt causing, high error rate generating topics in numeracy are long division and fractions (see Chapter 7). As I collect the data for the screening test that will be part of the companion book, *More Trouble with Maths* the frequency of 'no attempts' for the division items, $2\overline{)38}$, $10\overline{)6030}$ and $23 \div 1000$, is quite depressing. I could speculate as to why division creates so many issues for people by considering the skills, language and number fact knowledge required. The situation in the data collection for fractions is equally depressing. There are less 'no attempts' but a very low frequency of correct answers.

The illustrations that follow are not definitive lesson plans!

Division problems could be tackled immediately, an instant start, by implementing a procedure. However, this requires specific skills, predominantly based on memory. It may not require any understanding. As soon as one brings in understandings and more flexible approaches, such as estimating, then the student will require other prerequisite skills such as number sense and operations sense. This creates an impression in the learner that more time will be needed to reach the goal of an answer and that even more time will be needed to check the answer. Some learners will avoid such extra commitment even though it will create a skill that will be far more securely fixed in memory.

The whole situation around division and peoples' inability to solve problems is, for me, strong evidence against over-reliance on procedures.

What is division?

Fundamental questions are often a good place to start. It makes sense to assume that if you understand what you are doing you are more likely to do it correctly. If division is taught solely as a procedure, an algorithm, then the chances of it being forgotten are high. The task analysis below provides several reasons why this is so.

Division should be seen as part of a collection of four interconnected operations, addition, subtraction, multiplication and division. Addition seems to be the operation that is best understood and used most often. Division seems to be the operation that is least understood and avoided whenever possible!

```
          367
  73) 26791
      219
      489
      438
      511
      511
```

Figure 10.1 'Traditional' long division

There is a sequence in the inter-relationship between the four operations:

+ Addition starts with counting on in ones and moves to counting on in 'chunks' (in this case, numbers greater than one).

− Subtraction starts with counting back in ones and moves to counting back in 'chunks'. It is the opposite operation to addition.

× Multiplication is the repeated addition of the same number, that is, the same number is added repeatedly. The number can be added in 'chunks', for example, if the multiplying number is 17, then ten seventeens could be added in one step as 170.

÷ Division is the repeated subtraction of the same number, that is, the same number is subtracted repeatedly. The number can be subtracted in chunks, for example, if the dividing number is 17, then ten seventeens could be subtracted in one step as 170. Division is the opposite operation to multiplication.

Division by the traditional method (Figure 10.1) makes several demands. Let's do a task analysis in order to understand what we are asking of the learner.

Pupils need:

- an understanding of place value;
- an understanding of the symbols;
- an understanding of what division means;
- an understanding of the vocabulary (for example, 'How many seventeens in 113?');
- division facts for many numbers, including those that are not whole number multiples;
- estimation skills, for example, to be able to estimate how many times 17 goes into 113;
- sequencing skills for the steps in the procedure;
- organisation of work on paper;
- subtraction skills;
- understanding (try explaining the traditional long division procedure in terms of what is happening mathematically! Not impossible, but it can take a while).

However if it has to be taught – and some countries are deciding not to teach long division – try to decide which of the above factors are the most problematic for the pupil. As (almost) ever, ask the student to talk through what he knows and understands (meta-cognition).

If it is the ability to work out the factors, for example in $1139 \div 17$ the student will need to be able to compute 6×17 and 7×17, to have pre-estimated that these are the relevant factors for this question and know that it is the lower number, not the closer number, that has to be used.

This could be overcome by the setting up of a table of multiples. Set up the multiples in bold font first.

1 × 17 = 17	Encourage the use of inter-relationships.
2 × 17 = 34	This reduces the chance of cumulative errors.
3 × 17 = 51	
4 × 17 = 68	4 × 17 is twice 2 × 17
5 × 17 = 85	5 × 17 is half of 10 × 17
6 × 17 = 102	6 × 17 is 5 × 17 plus 17
7 × 17 = 119	7 × 17 is 5 × 17 plus 2 × 17 (85 + 34)
8 × 17 = 136	8 × 17 is 2 × 4 × 17
9 × 17 = 153	9 × 17 is 10 × 17 minus 17. Add the digits . . . they should add up to 9 (1 + 5 + 3 = 9).
10 × 17 = 170	Use place value knowledge.

This table will then support the traditional algorithm (procedure).

If it is subtraction skills that are a problem, then use the interchange of operations, so multiples of 17 can be added until the target number is reached. So, 1139 ÷ 17 becomes

$n \times 17 = 1139$, that is 'What do I have to multiply 17 by to get 1139?'

Encourage initial estimating by looking at the values of the numbers and exploring possibilities, for example, try $17 \times 10 = 170$, which is much too small so move to 17×100 which is 1700, which is too big, but not that far away, so the answer should lie between 50 and 100. That deduction requires the ability to appraise the estimates and gauge their distance away from the target answer.

Start with **50**:

$50 \times 17 = 850$

This is not enough so add on another **10** lots of 17 (170)

$850 + 170 = 1020$

Another 10 lots of 17 will go beyond the target 1139 to 1190, so try $\mathbf{5} \times 17 = 85$

$1020 + 85 = 1105$
add on **2** more 17s to reach 1139

Add up all the added $\boldsymbol{n} \times$ 17s

$\mathbf{50 + 10 + 5 + 2 = 67}$

If this is set up without the explanations, it looks like:

$50 \times 17 = 850$
$10 \times 17 = 170$
1020
$10 \times 17 = 170$
(too big) 1190

(back one step)

$60 \times 17 = 1020$
$5 \times 17 = 85$
1105
$2 \times 17 = 34$
so $67 \times 17 = \mathbf{1139}$

If subtraction skills are not problem, but the actual sequence of the traditional division procedure is the problem, either in terms of memory or spatial organisation, then a table of key value multipliers can be set up first:

$1 \times 17 = 17$
$2 \times 17 = 34$
$4 \times 17 = 68$
$5 \times 17 = 85$
$10 \times 17 = 170$ then follow the pattern based on $20 \times 17 = 10 \times 2 \times 17$, etc.
$20 \times 17 = 340$ this makes a 'built-in' check for multiples
$40 \times 17 = 680$
$50 \times 17 = 850$
$100 \times 17 = 1700$

Now divide by subtracting in (partial products or chunks) multiples of 17:

$$
\begin{array}{rr}
 & 1139 \\
\mathbf{50} \times 17 & -850 \\
\hline
 & 289 \\
\mathbf{10} \times 17 & -170 \\
\hline
 & 119 \\
\mathbf{5} \times 17 & -85 \\
\hline
 & 34 \\
\mathbf{2} \times 17 & -34 \\
\hline
\mathbf{67} & 0
\end{array}
$$

The subtraction method above is close to the traditional algorithm for long division, but makes less spatial demands, is more logical and links division to repeated subtraction (or subtraction in chunks or partial products). It uses multiples that are easier to compute.

These methods also teach further understanding of numbers and number operations.
Remember that there is never a universal method, a method that suits all learners.
Teaching is about responding to each learner.

Adding and subtracting fractions

Let's start with a method that does not teach anything else except how to add and subtract, mechanically, fractions.

A functional approach to be used only as a last ditch strategy

When explanations of the finer points of fractions are failing and deep meaningful understanding is a distant goal and GCSEs are two terms away I go for the instrumental approach (and thus abandoning developmental principles and teaching for under-standing). The methods are extreme inchworm. Note that it is often the pressure to achieve results in exams that drives teachers and learners to use procedures and algorithms.

The method involves classifying addition and subtraction of fractions into Types 1, 2 and 3. The focus is on the denominator, the bottom number and the number that confuses and creates errors, of each fraction, asking the questions:

- Are they the same? Yes. Type 1 for example, $\frac{2}{5} + \frac{3}{5}$.
- Is one a factor (or a multiple) of the other? Yes. Type 2 for example, $\frac{2}{5} + \frac{1}{10}$.
- Are they mathematically unrelated? Yes. Type 3 for example, $\frac{2}{5} + \frac{3}{7}$.

(Note: Type 2 can be treated as a Type 3, but the answer will have to be simplified.)

Type 1 . . . 'Same bottom line'

For example:

$$\frac{1}{5} + \frac{3}{5} = \frac{4}{5}$$

If the numbers on the bottom line (denominators, but how many pupils are going to forget or confuse that word) are the same, then you add (or subtract) the top numbers and the bottom numbers stay the same, hence reinforcing '*same* bottom line'.

Type 2 . . . 'Goesinto'

For example:

$$\frac{1}{2} + \frac{1}{4} = \frac{3}{4}$$

$$\frac{3}{20} + \frac{2}{5} = ?$$

Look at the bottom numbers . . . 2 goes into 4 and 5 goes into 20.
Both examples are Type 2. Thus the pupil needs to be able to know that one denominator is divisible by the other. If they are not factors move to Type 3.

So . . . if the bottom numbers of the fractions are divisible, do the division. For example:

$$4 \div 2 = 2 \text{ and } 20 \div 5 = 4$$

This gives the 'Goesinto number'.
Then the fraction with the smaller bottom number, in these cases 2 and 5 respectively, is multiplied by the 'Goesinto number' written as $\frac{n}{n}$.

$$\frac{1}{2} \times \frac{2}{2} = \frac{2}{4}$$

$$\frac{2}{5} \times \frac{4}{4} = \frac{8}{20}$$

This now becomes a Type 1:

$$\frac{2}{4} + \frac{1}{4} = \frac{3}{4}$$

$$\frac{3}{20} + \frac{8}{20} = \frac{11}{20}$$

The familiar $\frac{1}{2} + \frac{1}{4}$ example acts as a reminder of the Type 2 method.

Type 3 ... 'Doesn't gointo'

In Type 3 fractions the two denominators (bottom numbers) are not multiples or factors of each other, for example:

$$\frac{2}{3} - \frac{2}{5} =$$

$$\frac{3}{10} + \frac{5}{9} =$$

Appraisal of the bottom numbers shows that . . .
3 does not 'go into' 5 and 5 does not 'go into' 3
10 does not 'go into' 9 and 9 does not 'go into' 10

So these are Type 3 fraction problems.

The procedure is simple and involves multiplying (twice) diagonally across the + or − sign (criss-cross) and then multiplying the denominators (times).

$$\frac{3}{5} + \frac{2}{11} = \frac{33}{55} + \frac{10}{55} = \frac{43}{55}$$

Figure 10.2 The criss-cross-times method for fractions

The Types 1, 2 and 3 methods are purely mechanical, but do focus attention on the denominators. Type 3 has the benefit of a mnemonic ('criss-cross-times'). The labels also act as reminders to focus initially on the bottom number, the denominator.

Adding and subtracting fractions: a little more understanding

There are a number of misconceptions that handicap pupils' understanding of this topic. If the misconceptions are actively and positively acknowledged then the embedded problems they create may be pre-empted.

● There is a language and symbol factor in fractions. I asked a highly intelligent pupil 'What is half of fifty?' The almost instant answer was 'twenty-five'. A little while later I presented the student with a sheet of paper on which I had written:

$$\frac{1}{2} \times 50$$

She could not provide an answer, so I asked, 'Is the answer bigger or smaller than 50?' and she said 'Yes' (see also Chapter 1).
● There is a move away from previous experience where × meant getting a bigger answer. A new interpretation of multiplication is needed. I am always impressed by the fact that multiplications such as $\frac{2}{5} \times \frac{3}{7}$ give an answer that is smaller than either fraction. The rule is that when a multiplication is by a fraction which has a value of less than 1 the answer is smaller, so for $\frac{2}{5} \times \frac{3}{7}$, both fractions are less than 1 so the answer must be smaller than both $\frac{2}{5}$ and $\frac{3}{7}$.

- Another misconception (again language) is that a fraction is a single entity to be treated like any other number. Compare the vocabulary:

  sixth, six   tenth, ten   two sevenths, twenty-seven

  The vocabulary is too similar to suggest there is any radical difference. Then there is 'sixth' as being 'sixth in a race' and 'sixth' as $\frac{1}{6}$ to add more confusion.

- Add and subtract has always applied to the numbers on each side of the sign $+$ or $-$, so

  $$4 + 6 = 10 \text{ and } 16 - 9 = 7$$

  The misconception is that this continues to be the case with fractions, that is, add means add and subtract means subtract, so mistakes are made, such as:

  $$\frac{1}{2} + \frac{1}{2} = \frac{2}{4}$$

  $$\frac{9}{10} - \frac{3}{7} = \frac{6}{3}$$

  For fractions the $+$ and $-$ symbols now only apply selectively, that is to the top numbers (numerators).

- A particular value fraction may take many forms. The most common example of a fraction is half, $\frac{1}{2}$. For an hour, half is $\frac{30}{60}$. For a pound or a dollar or a Euro, half is $\frac{50}{100}$. For a kilogram, half is $\frac{500}{1000}$. For a year, it is $\frac{6}{12}$ or $\frac{26}{52}$. For a day it is $\frac{12}{24}$. For a mile it is $\frac{880}{1760}$. And so on. While pupils usually accept this for a half, it may be difficult for them to transfer that belief or concept or understanding to other fractions, such as a third or a seventh.

- This is a good example of the maths being easy until it has to be written down (as my friend and colleague Richard Ashcroft says). Asking 'What is a book plus a book?' is likely to elicit the answer, 'Two books' followed by 'What is a ninth plus a ninth?' which then is likely to elicit the answer 'Two ninths', but $\frac{1}{9} + \frac{1}{9}$ presented as written symbols is likely to result in $\frac{2}{18}$.

- A further issue is that multiplying by a fraction involves both denominator and numerator. When renaming fractions for addition or subtraction, the learner has to remember that $+$ and $-$ only applies to top numbers and that $\times$ applies to both the top and bottom numbers.

Building the foundations

The first foundation is to understand why a fraction is written the way it is, that is two numbers, one on top of the other and separated by a line. A fraction involving two digits, such as $\frac{2}{3}$ is very different to a number with two digits, such as 32.

A learner has to know that for 32, the 2 is 2 units and the 3 is 3 $\times$ 10, 3 tens. The multiplication symbol is hidden. Fractions are about division so a fraction could be visualised as incorporating a hidden division sign (Figure 10.3).

The golden rule of adding or subtracting fractions is that you can only start the addition or subtraction process when the fractions have been adjusted to have the same name (or denominator or bottom number). So, for example $\frac{1}{2} + \frac{1}{4}$ cannot be computed until the $\frac{1}{2}$ is renamed to be $\frac{2}{4}$, then

$$\frac{2}{4} + \frac{1}{4} = \frac{3}{4}$$

Figure 10.3 The hidden division sign

So students need to be able to rename fractions, understand what this means and why we do it. This is the second foundation. Part of this understanding is to revisit the mantra that some may have learned, that is that multiplying by one does not change the number. For renaming fractions, multiplying by one does not change the value of a fraction, but it does change the way it looks, the numbers in the renamed fraction are different.

Renaming implies that there already is a name. The name of $\frac{1}{2}$ is 'a half'. The name of $\frac{1}{7}$ is 'a seventh'.

The name of $\frac{2}{5}$ is 'fifth' and there are two of them, hence 'two fifths'. So the name ('nom') comes from the de*nom*inator, the bottom number, the number at the bottom of the fraction, the number below the dividing line.

As much time as is needed should be spent on developing the concept and skill of renaming.

Renaming does what it says it does, it takes a fraction, for example one fifth, $\frac{1}{5}$, and gives it a new name, for example two tenths, $\frac{2}{10}$. It does NOT give it a new value. The new-named fraction must be an equivalent, same value, fraction. It remains the same value because it is multiplied by another fraction whose value is one (1), for example $\frac{2}{2}$.

Examples can be taken from everyday experiences such as half an hour as $\frac{30}{60}$ ($\frac{1}{2} \times \frac{30}{30}$), half a pound (£) as $\frac{50}{100}$ ($\frac{1}{2} \times \frac{50}{50}$). The renaming fraction always has the same number as numerator and denominator (top number and bottom number) because it has a value of 1.

Tactile materials such as Cuisenaire rods, poker chips or stacker counters (from Crossbow Education, see Appendix 2) are good to show the equivalence of fractions. Visual images to illustrate the concept could be by folding squares or circles of paper. The written symbols should always be shown alongside these concrete experiences.

Maybe it is worth using colours, one colour for the numerator and a different one for the denominator just to add focus to the fraction as having two number components. Or writing a big division sign ÷ on the board to remind learners that a fraction is a number divided by another number.

A problem could occur if learners have automatic recall of only a few number facts then this will handicap the extent of their ability to rename fractions, so this process will require a lot of carefully structured practice, with the focus on the process rather than on knowing all the basic facts. Or, give out table squares. Tracking down the columns gives equivalent fraction values. For example, tracking down the 3 column and the 4 column together produces 6 and 8, 9 and 12, 12 and 16, 15 and 20 and so on to 30 and 40.

A known or, at least, a familiar example should be used as a first model, such as:

$\frac{1}{2}$ to be renamed to have the same denominator as $\frac{1}{4}$
or $\frac{1}{3}$ to be renamed to have the same denominator as $\frac{1}{12}$ (using the familiar model of a clock again)

The overview/start up questions that should be asked are:

For $\frac{1}{2} + \frac{1}{4}$

- Do both fractions have to be renamed? Not if one denominator is a multiple of the other denominator. 4 is a multiple of 2 so only the half has to be renamed. Does this help with the renaming?
- What number is used to change the chosen fraction, the half?

It will be found by dividing the larger denominator (4) by the smaller denominator (2), which should give a whole number (2), thereby avoiding creating a fraction within a fraction! In this example the renaming factor is therefore 2.

The top *and* bottom numbers of the fraction that has to be renamed have to be multiplied by this factor. In this example:

$$\frac{1}{2} \times \frac{2}{2} = \frac{2}{4}$$

Thus the fraction remains the same value, it is still a half, but is renamed from being called *one half* to being called *two quarters*.

If both fractions have to be renamed, for example $\frac{2}{3}$ and $\frac{1}{4}$ to have a common (meaning the same) denominator (meaning bottom number).

So in:

$$\frac{2}{3} + \frac{1}{4}$$

- Both fractions have to be renamed, each to become equivalent fractions.
- The simplest, but not necessarily the most numerically elegant, is to take the two denominators (bottom numbers) as factors of the new denominator and multiply them, using the commutative property. So the new denominator becomes 3 × 4 and 4 × 3, that is 12.
- For renaming, the numerator (top number) and denominator BOTH have to be multiplied.

So $\frac{2}{3}$ is multiplied by $\frac{4}{4}$ to give $\frac{8}{12}$ and $\frac{1}{4}$ is multiplied by $\frac{3}{3}$ to give $\frac{3}{12}$. Since both fractions are now renamed and written as twelfths they can now be added:

$$\frac{8}{12} + \frac{3}{12} = \frac{11}{12}$$

The answer $\frac{11}{12}$ is less than 1 and a sketch or estimate will show this to be as expected.

A circle picture as in Figure 10.4 can be used for estimates and appraisals of fraction sums. A clock is a good model (another reason to use an analogue watch) for $\frac{1}{2}, \frac{1}{3}, \frac{1}{4}, \frac{1}{6}, \frac{1}{12}$ and for interrelating these fractions (Figure 10.5).

The process of 'mutual' renaming can be demonstrated with squares of paper. For example, the $\frac{2}{3}$ cannot be added to the $\frac{1}{4}$ because the fractions, the parts are not the same size (Figure 10.6). The first fraction, $\frac{2}{3}$, was created by dividing the square into three parts and using two of them. The second fraction, $\frac{1}{4}$, was created by dividing the square into four parts and using one of them.

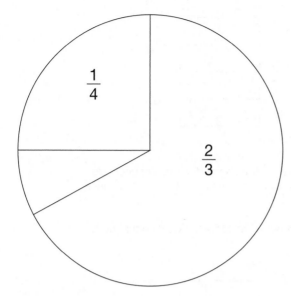

Figure 10.4 $\frac{1}{4} + \frac{2}{3}$

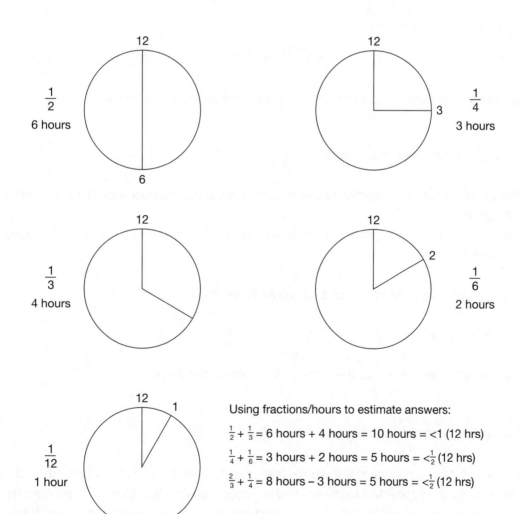

Using fractions/hours to estimate answers:

$\frac{1}{2} + \frac{1}{3}$ = 6 hours + 4 hours = 10 hours = <1 (12 hrs)

$\frac{1}{4} + \frac{1}{6}$ = 3 hours + 2 hours = 5 hours = $<\frac{1}{2}$ (12 hrs)

$\frac{2}{3} + \frac{1}{4}$ = 8 hours − 3 hours = 5 hours = $<\frac{1}{2}$ (12 hrs)

Figure 10.5 Fractions and clocks

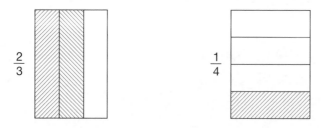

The $\frac{1}{3}$ fraction part is not the same size as the $\frac{1}{4}$ fraction part, so you cannot add them together as they are. They both need to be renamed so that they both have the same name.

So the third has to be quartered and the quarter has to be 'thirded' so that both become twelfths

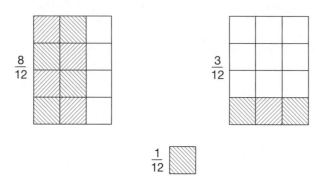

$\frac{1}{12}$ ▨

Figure 10.6 Renaming fractions to make them have the same name

To make both parts the same:

● the one divided into 3 parts initially is further divided, but into 4 parts (3 × 4 parts = 12 parts);
● the one divided into 4 parts initially is further divided, but into 3 parts (4 × 3 parts = 12 parts).

It's another example of the commutative property:

$a \times c = c \times a$

and once again we return to the basic principles of numbers.

Multiplication of fractions

The use of the paper square above returns to the two dimensional model for multiplication. If you wanted to demonstrate $\frac{2}{3} \times \frac{3}{4}$, then a little paper folding could help.

First divide the paper into thirds and fold back to show $\frac{2}{3}$. Turn the paper through 90° and fold it into quarters and fold back to show $\frac{3}{4}$ of the $\frac{2}{3}$. Unfold to show the resulting area is $\frac{6}{12}$ (then show that $\frac{6}{12}$ is $\frac{1}{2}$ and thus smaller than either $\frac{3}{4}$ or $\frac{2}{3}$). Unfold completely to show that the folding created twelfths.

Or prepare a PowerPoint presentation.

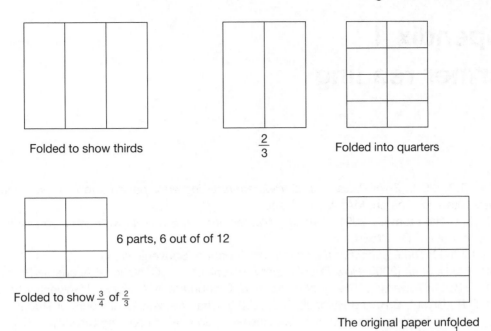

Folded to show thirds

$\frac{2}{3}$

Folded into quarters

6 parts, 6 out of of 12

Folded to show $\frac{3}{4}$ of $\frac{2}{3}$

The original paper unfolded
to show twelfths $\frac{1}{12}$

Figure 10.7 Folding paper to show $\frac{2}{3} \times \frac{3}{4} = \frac{6}{12} = \frac{1}{2}$

Conclusion

There is always more than one way to present information and to explain a maths topic. This chapter illustrates, for adding and subtracting fractions, the extremes of a purely instrumental, procedure-based method to a conceptual model based on the area theme that can be used so widely in many other topics in basic numeracy. It also shows how methods for division can be adapted to acknowledge more empathetically the skills and deficits of the learner.

Appendix 1
Further reading

Ashlock, R.B. (2009) *Error Patterns in Computation: Using error patterns to help each student learn*, 10th edn, Boston, MA: Allyn & Bacon.

Bley, N. and Thornton, C. (2001) *Teaching Mathematics to Students with Learning Disabilities*, 4th edn. Austin, TX: ProEd.

Boaler, J. (2009) *The Elephant in the Classroom*, London: Souvenir Press.

Bransford, J.D. *et al.* (2000) *How People Learn*, Washington, DC: National Academy Press.

Bruner, J. (1966) *Towards a Theory of Instruction*, Cambridge, MA: Harvard University Press.

Bryant, D.P., Bryant, B.R. and Hammill, D.D. (2000) 'Characteristic behaviours of students with LD who have teacher-identified math weaknesses', *Journal of Learning Disabilities*, 33, no. 2, 168–177, 199.

Butterworth, B. (1999) *The Mathematical Brain*, London: Papermac.

Chinn, S.J. (1997) *What to Do When You Can't Learn the Times Tables*, Wakefield: Egon Press.

Chinn, S.J. (2007) *Dealing with Dyscalculia: Sum Hope2*, London: Souvenir Press.

Chinn, S.J. (forthcoming) *More Trouble with Maths: A teacher's complete guide to identifying and diagnosing mathematical dfficulties*. London: Routledge.

Chinn, S.J. and Ashcroft, J.R. (2007) *Mathematics for Dyslexics Including Dyscalculia*, 3rd edn. Chichester: Wiley.

Clausen-May, T. (2005) *Teaching Maths to Pupils with Different Learning Styles*, London: Paul Chapman.

Deboys, M. and Pitt, E. (1979) *Lines of Development in Primary Mathematics*, Belfast: Blackstaff Press.

Devlin, K. (2000) *The Maths Gene*, London: Weidenfeld & Nicolson.

Dehaene, S. (1999) *The Number Sense: How the mind creates mathematics*, London: Penguin Books.

Dowker, A. (2005) *Individual Differences in Arithmetic*, Hove: Psychology Press.

Gathercole, S.E. and Packiam Alloway, T. (2008) *Working Memory and Learning*, London: Sage.

Geary, D. (1994) *Children's Mathematical Development*, Washington, DC: American Psychological Association.

Grauberg, E. (1998) *Elementary Mathematics and Language Difficulties*, London: Whurr.

Hattie, J. (2009) *Visible Learning*, London: Routledge.

Martin, H. (1996) *Multiple Intelligences in the Mathematics Classroom*, Arlington Heights, IL: IRI/Skylight Training.

McGrath, C. (2010) *Supporting Early Mathematical Development: Practical approaches to play-based learning*, London: Routledge.

Miles, T. and Miles, E. (eds) (2003) *Dyslexia and Mathematics*. 2nd edn, London: Routledge.

Skemp, R.R. (1986) *The Psychology of Learning Mathematics*, London: Penguin.

Thompson, I. (1999) *Issues in Teaching Numeracy in Primary Schools*, Buckingham: OUP.

Westwood, P. (2004) *Numeracy and Learning Difficulties*, London: Fulton.

Yeo, D. (2002) *Dyslexia, Dyspraxia and Mathematics*, London: Whurr (Wiley).

Appendix 2
Checklists and resources

Checklist for choosing a textbook

- Is the level of maths difficulty suitable?
- Is the language level suitable?
- Is the language clear, unambiguous and concise?
- Are there diagrams that actually aid learning?
- Is the layout of the page clear and well spaced?
- Is there some 'real' maths content?
- Are the worked examples clearly, simply, concisely and flexibly explained?
- Are the exercises/questions presented clearly?
- Is the progression in difficulty in the exercises/questions smooth and without any quantum leaps?
- Can the exercises be easily modified for differentiation?
- Is key information highlighted?

Checklist for modifying a worksheet to differentiate for a student

A simple, informal diagnosis of the student will lead to suggestions for differentiation. For example, reading accuracy and comprehension data will indicate the complexity of text the student can access (but remember that maths has its own vocabulary and unique semantics).

- Are the items/questions accessible to a poor reader? Check by looking at the vocabulary and language levels.
- Are new and key words explained on the sheet or have they been explained when the sheet was handed out?
- Are the numbers used, in at least the first few questions, accessible – that is, enough 1s, 2s, 5s whenever possible?
- Is there a quantum leap somewhere in the progression of difficulty?
- Are questions lined off to make them more distinct and less easy to mix up?
- Could diagrams be added to help the student's comprehension?
- Are there any examples to show how questions can be done and/or is there a summary of the main points tested in the questions?
- Have an appropriate number and range of questions been selected off the main worksheet?
- Can the layout be expanded so the student can answer on the worksheet (and thus eliminate copying and some writing)?
- Is it possible for the student to do and have marked the first two examples before taking the sheet away to attempt the remaining examples?

© 2012 Steve Chinn, *The Trouble with Maths*, London: Routledge.

● Have you checked for pitfalls and pre-empted them? (Or do you want your student to fall?!)

Test publishers and suppliers

GL Assessment: www.gl-assessment.co.uk
Hodder Education: www.hoddereducation.co.uk
Pearson Assessment: www.psychcorp.co.uk
Pro-Ed (USA): www.proedinc.com

Coloured overlays

Crossbow Education: www.crossboweducation.co.uk

Suppliers of software

AVP: www.avp.co.uk
Iansyst: www.iansyst.co.uk
REM: www.r-e-m.co.uk
White Space (for Number Shark): www.wordshark.co.uk

Evaluation questions for software

● Does it offer what you want – practice, learning, remedial intervention, extension or production (such as drawing graphs and charts)?
● Is it just a book on screen?
● Is the design cluttered?
● Is there mathematical structure?
● Is it just drill and kill?
● Does it irritate?
● Does it have voice output?
● How does it motivate, success and/or entertainment?
● Is it age-specific in design?
● Does it address more than one way of learning?
● Is it good value for money?
● Can the learner use it independently?
● Does it have a record-keeping system?
● Can the programme be individualised?
● Do users always have to start at the beginning or can they dip in at any point?
● Does it include assessment and/or diagnostic features?

© 2012 Steve Chinn, *The Trouble with Maths*, London: Routledge.

Appendix 3
'Jog your memory cards' for multiplication facts

2 × 7 = **14**	5 × 7 = **35**	2 × 8 = **16**	5 × 8 = **40**	1 × 8 = **8**
2 × 6 = **12**	5 × 6 = **30**	1 × 6 = **6**	1 × 7 = **7**	Use the 'easy' nine to work out the 'tough' fourteen
Use two cards to work out one fact	HOW TO USE THE EASY NINE Example for 6 × 8 use two cards … use 5 × 8 = 40 and 1 × 8 = 8 to give 6 × 8 = 48 (which is also 8 × 6)	**8 × 8** = **8×2×2×2** = 16 32 **64**	the 'tough' fourteen 6 × 6 6 × 7 7 × 6 6 × 8 8 × 6 7 × 7 7 × 8 8 × 7 3 × 6 6 × 3 3 × 7 7 × 3 3 × 8 8 × 3	
'jym' cards jog your memory cards		3x8 = 2x8 + 1x8 = 8x3 6x8 = 5x8 + 1x8 = 8x6 7x8 = 5x8 + 2x8 = 8x7	3x6 = 2x6 + 1x6 = 6x3 6x6 = 5x6 + 1x6 7x6 = 5x6 + 2x6 = 6x7	3x7 = 2x7 + 1x7 = 7x3 6x7 = 5x7 + 1x7 = 7x6 7x7 = 5x7 + 2x7

© 2012 Steve Chinn, *The Trouble with Maths*, London: Routledge.

1 × 2 = 2 **2 × 2 = 4** **3 × 2 = 6** **4 × 2 = 8** 5 × 2 = 10 **6 × 2 = 12** **7 × 2 = 14** **8 × 2 = 16** **9 × 2 = 18** 10 × 2 = 20	**Using the first half of the 2× table to work out the second half**	**2 × 2** **=** **4**
5 × 2 **=** **10**	**1 × 2** **=** **2**	**3 × 2** **=** **6**

4 × 2
=
 	
8
	6 = 5 + 1
	7 = 5 + 2
	8 = 5 + 3
	9 = 5 + 4
	
	Use two cards to work out one fact
		Examples:
		6 × 2 = 5 × 2 + 1 × 2
		         = 10 + 2
		         = 12
		8 × 2 = 5 × 2 + 3 × 2
		         = 10 + 6
		         = 16
		9 × 2 = 5 × 2 + 4 × 2
		         = 10 + 8
		         = 18
		Now work out 7 × 2

© 2012 Steve Chinn, *The Trouble with Maths*, London: Routledge.

7 5 + 2	6 5 + 1	3 2 + 1
4 2 × 2	**9** 10 − 1	*8* *2 × 2 × 2* **10 − 2**
The links *3 = 2 + 1* *4 = 2 × 2* *6 = 5 + 1* *7 = 5 + 2* *8 = 2 × 2 × 2* *9 = 10 − 1*	**Linking the 'hard' numbers to the 'easy' numbers.**	

© 2012 Steve Chinn, *The Trouble with Maths*, London: Routledge.

1 × 2 = 2	1 × 10 = 10	1 × 5 = ~~10~~ 5
2 × 2 = 4	2 × 10 = 20	2 × 5 = ~~20~~ 10
3 × 2 = 6	3 × 10 = 30	3 × 5 = ~~30~~ 15
4 × 2 = 8	4 × 10 = 40	4 × 5 = ~~40~~ 20
~~5 × 2 = 10~~	5 × 10 = 50	5 × 5 = ~~50~~ 25
6 × 2 = 12	6 × 10 = 60	6 × 5 = ~~60~~ 30
7 × 2 = 14	7 × 10 = 70	7 × 5 = ~~70~~ 35
8 × 2 = 16	8 × 10 = 80	8 × 5 = ~~80~~ 40
9 × 2 = 18	9 × 10 = 90	9 × 5 = ~~90~~ 45
~~10 × 2 = 20~~	10 × 10 = 100	10 × 5 = ~~100~~ 50

1 × 9 = ~~10~~ 9	2 × 1 = 2	5 × 1 = 5
2 × 9 = ~~20~~ 18	2 × 2 = 4	5 × 2 = 10
3 × 9 = ~~30~~ 27	2 × 3 = 6	5 × 3 = 15
4 × 9 = ~~40~~ 36	2 × 4 = 8	2 × 4 = 20
5 × 9 = ~~50~~ 45	~~2 × 5 = 10~~	5 × 5 = 25
6 × 9 = ~~60~~ 54	2 × 6 = 12	5 × 6 = 30
7 × 9 = ~~70~~ 63	2 × 7 = 14	5 × 7 = 35
8 × 9 = ~~80~~ 72	2 × 8 = 16	5 × 8 = 40
9 × 9 = ~~90~~ 81	2 × 9 = 18	5 × 9 = 45
10 × 9 = 90	~~2 × 10 = 20~~	5 × 10 = 50

THE 'EASY' TABLES

1

2 ×

5 ×

10 ×

REMEMBER

THE ORDER OF MULTIPLYING CAN BE SWAPPED

examples:

4 × 6 = 6 × 4

8 × 7 = 7 × 8

3 × 9 = 9 × 3

© 2012 Steve Chinn, *The Trouble with Maths*, London: Routledge.

Appendix 4
Setting an inclusive maths department policy

General principles

All work must be modified appropriately to enable included pupils to succeed and achieve the maximum levels of which they are capable. Proactive intervention could be seen to be at three broad levels:

1 Simple adjustments to lessons, which include giving instructions that will not overload poor short-term memory, repetition of instructions (aural) reinforced by board work (visual).
2 More directed intervention, which might include seating a pupil where he can see the board clearly, hear and see the teacher properly, basic modifications to written material, for example selecting fewer examples for the pupil to complete, checking early on in individual work to ensure he has started and is doing the work correctly.
3 Individual intervention, which may include a specially modified worksheet, using a bigger font, different coloured paper, using a learning support assistant who has been briefed on how to intervene for the topic being taught.

To achieve the goal of maximising the success of the included special needs child or the uncertain learner (who may never carry a label) the following factors will be acknowledged and positive adjustments will be made to all teaching.

Consistency

Insecure learners like as much of the structure and arrangements around lessons to be as consistent as is possible. For example, in a mental arithmetic session, set a pattern of asking the child a question, so the question does not catch him unawares. Perhaps flag up the question, ask another pupil another question and then return to re-ask the question. Perhaps ask a part question. Make your strategy a routine.

Multisensory and developmental work

There are several reasons why work needs to be presented in a multisensory way and with a developmental structure.

● Some pupils always need to start with the concrete and can then move to the symbolic and on to the abstract. It is usually better if the materials chosen to represent the concept have consistency (see above), for example, the area model.
● Some pupils are visual learners.

● Work should always be developmental to give slower learners the best chance of reducing the performance gap. This includes referring the current topic back to an earlier level and checking on the foundations of the topic. This also acts as revision and review.

Language factors

Although it may seem to be stating the obvious, language must be kept clear and simple. This is not just the 'louder and slower' technique, but an intellectual appraisal of the vocabulary and sentence structures used in instruction. This includes dealing with new vocabulary and any dual meaning vocabulary, such as 'take away' for 'subtraction'.

Presentation issues, spoken and written

The factors that the learner brings to presentation by the teacher are short-term memory, pragmatic language skills and reading skills. The teacher can accommodate these as far as is possible in the structure of the lesson, including clear and uncluttered board work, and straightforward clear language that sticks to the point.

Safe learning and risk

Learners must feel safe to ask questions and know they will not be ridiculed (even mildly) and feel safe to make a start on questions, even though their initial work may be very wide of the best procedure.

Pupil involvement and interactions

Insecure learners may quietly withdraw mentally from lessons, just sitting unobtrusively at the back of the class. They need to be drawn, empathetically, into the lesson. Quiet pupils deserve as much attention as the noisy pupils.

Structured for revisions, reviews and recaps

The curriculum must be structured for revision. Any extension of a previously studied topic must be preceded by a review of the work so far and then summarised at the end of the lesson. (Remember that old adage, 'Tell them what you are going to teach, teach it and tell them what you have just taught.')

Structured for success

Genuine success is a motivating influence. Work should be structured and presented in small steps that encourage success and do not suddenly face learners with insurmountable hurdles (but don't forget this approach may need to be modified for grasshoppers). This requires a lot of checking of all work given to pupils. Assuming that an exercise is suitable without actually working it through is not acceptable.

Relevant

Whenever possible, the work must be shown to be relevant. Building in relevance is a good subject for departmental discussions.

Speed and pace

It is important to remember that the speed at which pupils do maths may be yet another example of normal distribution. It would be educationally immoral to ignore either extreme of that distribution. This applies to both mental arithmetic and written problems.

Empathetic teaching

This could be the only consideration in that it summarises all the others. Empathy implies an understanding of the learner and all that he brings to a lesson, from attitude and anxiety to mathematical memory to problem solving skills and proactively acknowledging those attributes in the way you teach.

Responsive

Many modern teaching schemes for numeracy encourage children to explore different methods of solving problems. This acknowledges that the most appropriate method for an individual pupil may be individual to that pupil. Teaching should be responsive to the learner and the way he learns and thinks, his attitude and interests, which implies that teachers must be aware of the way each learner learns and what he, the learner, brings to each lesson.

Learning and thinking styles

Following on from responsive teaching is a need to be aware of the learning styles and the thinking styles of each pupil in each classroom, in particular those pupils whose thinking styles are at the extremes of the continuum.

Marking, feedback and praise

Learners' attributions will be influenced by the feedback they receive in lessons, whether it is verbal or written comments used in marked work. Dramatic use of red pens is banned, indeed any red marking is banned. Try discrete marking in green.

Check new work early

Before an error pattern is internalised by the learner.

Teach patterns

Do not assume that all learners will automatically 'discover' the pattern, idea or concept that you, the teacher are so artfully guiding them towards. Sometimes it is best to know the final destination in order to appreciate the route taken.
   Finally,

   Do not assume . . .

   It may also be a good exercise for a Mathematics Department to set up its own key principles of teaching mathematics, for example:

Basic principles of teaching mathematics

Vocabulary

Make sure that *all* vocabulary is understood and placed in a mathematical context, e.g. 'take away' means 'subtract' in mathematics.

Language

Mathematics has its own language. It is not just the ability to read the words, but the ability to comprehend the maths meaning, for example, 'Remove the brackets' $(y + 3)$ $(y - 5)$ is not meant literally. Ensure the pupil is focused on the mathematical meaning.

The big picture and details

Grasshoppers will appreciate the outline of the whole picture, but need to learn to notice detail and to document their methods. Inchworms need to learn to overview and see the big picture. Putting the concept into a 'real' situation and linking the maths to previous experiences benefits both thinking styles.

Relate to other maths topics

Revise and build. (This includes taking every opportunity to reinforce number skills.)

Easy numbers

Use the 'easy' numbers to illustrate the first worked examples and in the first practise of independent examples. Focus on the concept, not on the number facts.

Quick check

Mark the first two practise examples before allowing further progress so the learner's error patterns do not become embedded in memory.

Speed

Remember that some pupils take longer to do work, so select fewer examples for them, but make sure these still cover the range of necessary experience (and look out for quantum leaps that occur in some sets of questions, where, for example, questions 1, 2 and 3 are straightforward and then, wham, question 4 leaps to degree level).

    Remember also that some pupils retrieve and process information more slowly, so make allowances for that.

Notes

1 Introduction: learning difficulties in mathematics and dyscalculia

1 Krutetskii, V.A. (1976) *The Psychology of Mathematical Abilities in Schoolchildren*, Chicago: University of Chicago Press.
2 Skemp, R.R. (1986) *The Psychology of Learning Mathematics*, London: Penguin, pp. 64, 78.
3 Butterworth, B. (2003) *The Dyscalculia Screener*, London: GL Assessment.
4 Chinn, S.J. (2003) 'Does dyscalculia add up?', *Dyslexia Review*, 14, no. 3.
5 Chinn, S.J. and Ashcroft, J.R. (2007) *Mathematics for Dyslexics: A teaching handbook*, 3rd edn, Chichester: Wiley.

3 What the curriculum asks pupils to do and where difficulties may occur

1 Bransford, J.D. *et al.* (2000) *How People Learn*, Washington, DC: National Academy Press.
2 Bryant *et al.* (2000) 'Characteristic behaviors of students with learning disabilities who have teacher-identified math weaknesses', *Journal of Learning Disabilities*, 33, no. 2, 168–77.
3 Bransford, J.D. *et al.*, ibid.
4 Hattie, J. (2009) *Visible Learning*, London: Routledge.
5 Bransford, J. D., Brown, A. L. and Cocking, R. R. (2000) *How People Learn*, Washington, DC: National Academy Press.
6 For further details of methods for teaching addition, subtraction, multiplication and division, and other basic topics see Steve Chinn (2009) *What to Do When You Can't . . . Maths Books* (series), Wakefield: Egon Publishing.

4 Thinking styles and mathematics

1 Ofsted (2006) *Evaluation: Maths provision for 14–19-year-olds*, London: HM Stationery Office.
2 Skemp, R.R. (1986) *The Psychology of Learning Mathematics*, London: Penguin.
3 Usiskin, Z. (1988) 'Conceptions of school algebra and uses of variables', in Coxford, A. and Schulte, A.P. (eds) *Ideas of Algebra, K-12*, Reston, VA: NCTM.
4 Marolda, M.R. and Davidson, P.S. (2000) 'Mathematical learning styles and differentiated teaching strategies', *Perspectives* (International Dyslexia Association), 26, no. 3, 10–15.
5 Bransford, J.D. *et al.* (2000) *How People Learn*, Washington, DC: National Academy Press.
6 Hattie, J. (2009) *Visible Learning*, London: Routledge.
7 See Steve Chinn (forthcoming) *More Trouble with Maths: A teacher's complete guide to identifying and diagnosing mathematical difficulties*, London: Routledge.
8 National Council for Curriculm and Assessment (1999) *Mathematics Curriculum*, Dublin: NCCA.
9 The Curriculum Development Council (1999) *Syllabuses for Secondary Schools:* Mathematics, Hong Kong: The Education Department. Available at: http://cd1.edb.hkedcity.net/cd/maths/en/doc/curr_syll/Math_Syllabuses_eng_pdf/Math_Sec_1-5_1999_e.pdf (accessed 1 May 2011).
10 The CAME programme was developed at Kings College, London. For CAME curriculum materials, see Adhami, M., Shayer, M. and Twiss, S. (2005) *Let's Think through Maths! 6–9*, London: nferNelson.

5 Developmental perspectives

1 Chinn, S.J. and Ashcroft, J.R. (1993) *Mathematics for Dyslexics*, 1st edn.
2 Bransford, J.D. *et al.* (2000) *How People Learn*, Washington, DC: National Academy Press.
3 Gagne, R. (1970) *The Conditions of Learning*, New York: Holt, Rinehart & Winston.

6 The vocabulary and language of maths

1 Boaler, J. (2009) *The Elephant in the Classroom*, London: Souvenir Press.
2 Henderson, A. (1998) *Maths for the Dyslexic*, London: Fulton. See also Henderson, A. and Miles, E. (2001) *Basic Topics in Mathematics for Dyslexics*, London: Whurr.
3 Kho Tek Hong *et al.* (2009) *The Singapore Model Method for Learning Mathematics*, Singapore: Ministry of Education.
4 Henderson, ibid.

7 Anxiety and attributions

1 Seligman, M. (1998) *Learned Optimism*, New York: Pocket Books.
2 Chinn, S.J. (2009) 'Mathematics anxiety in secondary students in England', *DYSLEXIA*, 15, 61–8.
3 Hattie, J. (2009) *Visible Learning*, London: Routledge.
4 Burden, R. (2005) *Dyslexia and Self-concept: Seeking a dyslexic identity*, London: Wiley.
5 Hattie, ibid.

8 The inconsistencies of maths

1 Cialdini, R.B. (2007) *Influence: The psychology of persuasion*, New York: William Morrow, p. 61.
2 Hattie, J. (2009) *Visible Learning*, London: Routledge, p. 145.
3 See Skemp, R.R. (1986) *The Psychology of Learning Mathematics*, London: Penguin.
4 Buswell, G.T. and Judd, C.M. (1925) *Summary of Educational Investigations Relating to Arithmetic: Supplementary educational monographs*, Chicago: University of Chicago Press.
5 Chinn, S.J. (2001) 'It was just a matter of time', *Mathematics Teaching*, 175 (June), 12–13.

9 Manipulatives and materials: multisensory learning

1 Dearden, R.F. (1967), quoted in Cobb, P. (1991) 'Reconstructing secondary school mathematics', *Focus on Learning Problems in Mathematics*, 13, no. 2, 3–32.
2 Hart, K. (1989) (1989) 'There is little connection' in Ernest, P. (ed.) *Mathematics Teaching: The state of the art*, Lewes: The Falmer Press.
3 Kho Tek Hong *et al.* (2009) *The Singapore Model Method for Learning Mathematics*, Singapore: Ministry of Education.
4 Swan, P. and White, G. (2000s) *Hands-on Maths* (series), Wexford, Ireland: Prim-Ed.

Index

www.routledge.com/education

More Trouble with Maths
A teacher's complete guide to identifying and diagnosing mathematical difficulties

Steve Chinn, Education Consultant, UK

There are many factors that can contribute to the learning difficulties children and adults have with mathematics. These include poor working memory, difficulties in retrieving so-called 'basic' facts and the ability to remember and apply formulas and procedures correctly.

This highly practical teacher resource is for anyone who would like to accurately and effectively identify dyscalculia amongst their pupils. Written in an engaging and user-friendly style, Steve Chinn draws on his extensive experience and expertise and this book shows:

- how to consider all the factors relating to mathematical learning difficulties;
- how these factors can be investigated;
- their impact on learning;
- a range of tests ranging from pre-requisite skills such as working memory to a critique of normative tests for mathematics knowledge and skills.

The book will guide the reader in the interpretation of tests, emphasising the need for a clinical approach when assessing individuals, and shows how diagnosis and assessment can become part of everyday teaching. This resource also includes pragmatic tests which can be implemented in the classroom, and shows how identifying the barriers is the first step in setting up any programme of intervention.

978-0-415-67013-5
£45.00

For more information and to order a copy visit
www.routledge.com/9780415670135

Available from all good bookshops